All Color Book of
SOUPS AND APPETIZERS

ARCO PUBLISHING INC.
New York

CONTENTS

Series editor: Mary Lambert

Published 1984 by
Arco Publishing, Inc.
215 Park Avenue South
New York, NY 10003

© Marshall Cavendish Books Limited 1984

Library of Congress
Catalog Card Number: 84-70832
ISBN 0-668-06219-3 cloth
ISBN 0-668-06226-6 paper

Printed in Italy

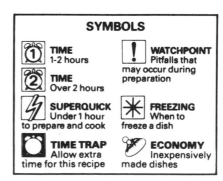

SYMBOLS

TIME 1-2 hours

TIME Over 2 hours

SUPERQUICK Under 1 hour to prepare and cook

TIME TRAP Allow extra time for this recipe

WATCHPOINT Pitfalls that may occur during preparation

FREEZING When to freeze a dish

ECONOMY Inexpensively made dishes

INTRODUCTION

Planning a balanced menu for a dinner party or a pleasant family meal is never easy and often it can be very difficult to find that right first course. This book on soups and appetizers gives you a wide range of inexpensive and quick recipes to choose from.

You can make a warm filling soup, a tasty pâté or maybe a more exotic seafood appetizer often using some ingredients you will already have on the pantry shelf. There are also a good selection of meat and vegetable recipes to give you that extra variety.

There are nearly 80 recipes and all are calorie counted, have full color pictures and contain cook's notes which give serving and buying ideas for the dish. They also tell you the timing of the dish and alternative fillings to make it more economic or perhaps to spice it up more.

SOUPS

Frankfurter and vegetable soup

SERVES 4

¼ lb frankfurters, cut into ¼-inch slices
2 tablespoons vegetable oil
⅓ lb carrots cut into ½-inch dice
1 celery stalk, thinly sliced
½ lb turnips, cut into ½-inch dice
1 onion, chopped
1 clove garlic, crushed (optional)
3 cups beef broth
1 can (about 14 oz) tomatoes, chopped
salt and freshly ground black pepper
¾ cup shredded green cabbage
1 tablespoon pasta (see Buying guide)
½ cup grated Cheddar cheese

1 Heat the oil in a heavy-based saucepan, add the carrots, celery, turnips, onion and garlic, if using, and cook for 7 minutes, stirring.
2 Remove from the heat and stir in the broth and tomatoes with juice. Season to taste with salt and pepper.
3 Return the pan to the heat and bring to a boil. Lower the heat, cover the pan and simmer for 20 minutes.
4 Add the cabbage and pasta, then cover again and simmer for a further 10 minutes until the pasta is soft.
5 Stir in the frankfurters, taste and adjust seasoning, and cook for a further 3 minutes.
6 Ladle into warmed individual bowls or a soup tureen and serve at once. Hand the grated cheese in a separate bowl for sprinkling on top of the soup.

Cook's Notes

TIME
Preparation takes 20 minutes, cooking 45 minutes.

BUYING GUIDE
Soup pasta, or pastina, as the Italians call it, comes in tiny star and circle shapes. If it is not available, use small pasta shapes or quick-cook pasta broken into ½-inch lengths.

VARIATION
Use potatoes or rutabagas in place of turnips.

FREEZING
Transfer to a rigid container, cool quickly, then seal, label and freeze for up to 6 months. To serve: Thaw at room temperature for 2-3 hours, then reheat thoroughly until bubbling.
Add a little more broth if necessary.

SERVING IDEAS
Serve this hearty soup with toast or whole wheat bread for a meal in itself.

● 250 calories per portion

Quick meat and potato soup

SERVES 4

1½ lb potatoes, diced
1 tablespoon vegetable oil
1 large onion, finely chopped
2½ cups chicken broth
salt and freshly ground black pepper
1 can (about 7 oz) corned beef, diced
1 can (about 7½ oz) whole kernel
  corn, drained
1 tablespoon chopped parsley

1 Heat the oil in a large saucepan, add the onion and cook gently for 2-3 minutes. Add the potatoes and cook for a further 1-2 minutes, stirring with a wooden spoon.
2 Stir the broth into the pan, season lightly with salt and pepper and bring to a boil. Lower the heat, cover and simmer for 10 minutes.
3 Add the corned beef and the corn, bring back to a boil, then lower the heat again and simmer for a further 10 minutes.
4 Stir in parsley, taste and adjust seasoning, then pour into warmed soup bowls. Serve at once.

Cook's Notes

TIME
This pantry-shelf meal-in-one soup is extremely quick to make: It can be ready to serve within 30 minutes.

VARIATIONS
Drained canned lima beans could be used instead of, or in addition to, the corn. Children like baked beans in this soup.

SERVING IDEAS
Serve with hot pita bread, wholewheat rolls or French bread.

BUYING GUIDE
Choose firm, waxy potatoes such as the Idaho type for this soup. Floury potatoes would not be suitable, as they tend to disintegrate.

● 350 calories per portion

Salami and tomato soup

SERVES 4

⅓ cup sliced, skinned and roughly
   chopped salami
1 tablespoon butter
¾ cup diced potatoes
¾ cup diced carrots
1 onion, roughly chopped
1 teaspoon paprika
1 can (about 8 oz) tomatoes, chopped
⅔ cup tomato juice
2 cups chicken broth
¼ teaspoon dried rosemary
salt and freshly ground white
   pepper
1 can (about 14 oz) navy beans
1 tablespoon chopped fresh parsley

SESAME CROUTONS

2 tablespoons butter, softened
1 tablespoon sesame seeds
1 teaspoon Dijon-style mustard
4 thick slices white bread, crusts
   removed

1 Melt the butter in a saucepan, add the potatoes, carrots, onion and paprika and cook gently for 5 minutes until the onions are soft.

2 Stir in the tomatoes and their juice, the tomato juice and broth then bring to a boil. Lower the heat, stir in the rosemary and season with salt and pepper. Cover and simmer for 20 minutes until the vegetables are tender.

3 Remove from the heat and leave to cool slightly, then purée in a blender or work through a sieve.

4 Make the croutons: Put the butter in a bowl and beat in the sesame seeds and mustard. Spread on one side of each slice of bread. Cut the bread into ¾-inch cubes and put them in a skillet. Cook gently for 5 minutes or until they are golden, turning frequently.

5 Return the soup to the rinsed-out pan and stir in the salami. ✳ Add the beans and heat through gently for 5 minutes, then taste and adjust the seasoning if necessary.

6 Ladle the soup into warmed individual bowls or a soup tureen, top with the sesame croutons and then sprinkle over the chopped parsley. Serve the soup at once.

Cook's Notes

TIME
Preparation takes 20 minutes and cooking about 25 minutes.

VARIATIONS
Use ham or garlic sausage instead of the salami. Red kidney beans or butter or lima beans could be used instead of navy beans.

ECONOMY
Use any left-over cooked meat such as pork or chicken for this recipe.

FOR CHILDREN
Use sliced frankfurters or cooked pork sausages instead of the salami.

FREEZING
Cool completely, then transfer to a rigid container. Seal, label and freeze for up to 3 months. To serve: Reheat from frozen, then stir in the beans and cook for a further 5 minutes while making the sesame croutons.

● 330 calories per portion

Spinach and liver pâté soup

SERVES 4

1 can (about 1 lb 12 oz) cream of chicken soup
½ lb chopped frozen spinach, thawed, or canned spinach, drained
¼ lb liver pâté (see Buying guide)
a little milk (optional)
2 teaspoons lemon juice
salt and freshly ground black pepper

TO GARNISH

2 tablespoons butter or margarine
4 slices bacon, chopped
2 slices white bread, crusts removed and cut into small dice

1 Make up the garnish: Melt the butter in a skillet. Add the bacon and cook briskly for 2-3 minutes to release any fat. Add the diced bread and cook over moderate to high heat until both bacon and bread are lightly browned and crisp. Drain the bacon and croutons well on paper towels and keep hot until serving.

2 Pour the soup into a large saucepan, add the spinach and heat very gently until the mixture is just simmering.

3 Using a wire whisk, gradually beat the liver pâté into the soup. If the soup seems too thick, add a small amount of milk. Add the lemon juice and season carefully with salt and pepper.

4 Serve the soup piping hot in warmed individual soup bowls, sprinkled with the crispy bacon pieces and the croutons.

Country soup

SERVES 4

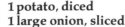

1 potato, diced
1 large onion, sliced
1 small head celery, sliced
¼ head firm cabbage, shredded
1 can (about 8 oz) tomatoes with
   juice
3¾ cups beef or ham broth
1 can (about 8 oz) kidney beans,
   drained
1 large or 2 medium frankfurter
   sausages
⅓ cup diced garlic sausage or
   salami
⅓ cup diced smoked sausage
salt and freshly ground black pepper
1 tablespoon finely chopped fresh
   parsley

1 Put the potato, onion, celery and cabbage in a large saucepan. Add the tomatoes with their juice, breaking them up against the sides of the pan with a wooden spoon.

2 Add the broth to the pan and bring quickly to a boil. Lower the heat to moderate, cover and simmer for 40 minutes.

3 Add the kidney beans, cover and cook for a further 20 minutes.

4 Meanwhile, bring a pan of water to a boil. Put the frankfurters into it and heat them through for 2 minutes. Remove with a slotted spoon and slice.

5 Add the garlic and smoked sausage and the frankfurters to the soup. Simmer over low heat for 15 minutes. Taste and adjust seasoning, [!] then pour into warmed individual soup bowls and sprinkle with chopped parsley. Serve at once.

Beefy soup

SERVES 4-6

1 lb lean ground beef
3 tablespoons shortening
2 onions, finely chopped
1 large potato, cut into ½-inch
  dice
1 large green pepper, seeded and cut
  into chunks
2 teaspoons paprika
2 tablespoons tomato paste
3¾ cups beef broth (see Cook's tip)
1 can (about 7 oz) whole kernel corn,
  drained
salt and freshly ground black
  pepper
⅔ cup dairy sour cream
1 tablespoon chopped chives

1 Melt shortening in a large saucepan, add the onions and potato and cook gently for about 5 minutes. Add the green pepper and cook for a further 10 minutes, stirring the vegetables occasionally to prevent them from sticking.

2 Sprinkle the paprika into the pan and cook for 1-2 minutes. Add the tomato paste and cooked beef, stirring with a wooden spoon to remove any lumps. Cook for 5 minutes, then pour in the beef broth and bring to a boil. Lower the heat and simmer for about 15 minutes, until the potatoes are tender.

3 Stir in the drained corn, heat through for 1-2 minutes, then taste and adjust seasoning if necessary.

4 Pour into warmed individual soup bowls. Top each serving with a swirl of sour cream, sprinkle with the chives and serve at once.

Mexican chili soup

SERVES 4

⅓–½ lb lean ground beef
1 tablespoon corn oil
1 large onion, chopped
½ teaspoon ground cumin
1½ tablespoons all-purpose flour
1 can (about 8 oz) tomatoes
½ teaspoon hot-pepper sauce (see Variations)
3¾ cups beef broth
salt and freshly ground black pepper
1 can (about 15 oz) red kidney beans, drained (see Variations)
fresh coriander or flat-leaved parsley, to garnish (optional)

1 Heat the oil in a saucepan and add the onion, ground beef and cumin. Cook over high heat until the meat is evenly browned, stirring with a wooden spoon to remove any lumps and mix thoroughly.
2 Sprinkle in the flour and stir well, then add the tomatoes with their juice, the pepper sauce and broth.
3 Bring to a boil, stirring. Season to taste with salt and pepper and simmer, uncovered, for 25 minutes.
4 Add the drained beans, stir them in and cook for a further 5 minutes or until heated through. Transfer to a warmed serving dish, sprinkle with coriander, if liked, then serve the soup at once (see Serving ideas).

Autumn soup

SERVES 4-6

1 large onion, chopped
2 carrots, cut into ½-inch dice
1 small rutabaga, peeled and cut into
 ½-inch dice
½ green pepper, seeded and thinly
 sliced
3 tablespoons vegetable oil
1 tablespoon tomato paste
3¾ cups beef broth
⅓ cup red lentils
salt and freshly ground black pepper
⅓ lb pork sausagemeat
½ cup fresh white bread crumbs
½ teaspoon chopped fresh
 rosemary, or 1 teaspoon dried
 rosemary
1 green apple
1 large potato, cut into ½-inch
 dice
chopped chives, to garnish

1 Heat the oil in a large flameproof casserole. Add the onion, carrots, rutabaga and green pepper and cook gently for 3 minutes until the vegetables are soft but not colored.
2 Stir in the tomato paste, broth and lentils, and season to taste with salt and pepper.
3 Bring to a boil, then lower the heat, cover and simmer for 20 minutes until the vegetables are just tender.
4 Meanwhile, put the sausagemeat, bread crumbs and rosemary in a bowl. Mix thoroughly with your hands, then shape into 12 small balls.
5 Pare and core the apple, then cut it into ½-inch dice. Add to the soup with the potato and sausage-meat balls and simmer for a further 25 minutes until all the vegetables are tender.
6 Taste and adjust seasoning, then serve hot, sprinkled with chives.

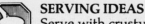

Cook's Notes

TIME
Preparation takes 20 minutes, cooking 50 minutes.

SERVING IDEAS
Serve with crusty bread or rolls as a main-meal soup for lunch. Sprinkle with grated cheese, if liked.

VARIATIONS
In place of the sausage-meat balls, dice ¼ lb skinned garlic sausage or salami and stir into the soup 10 minutes before the end of cooking. Pearl barley can be used instead of lentils, but you will need to allow at least another 30 minutes cooking time before adding the sausage-meat balls.

COOK'S TIP
To give the sausage-meat balls a golden-brown color cook them separately in a little oil, then add to the soup just before serving.

● 380 calories per portion

Mussel soup

SERVES 4

4½ pints fresh mussels (see Buying guide and Preparation)
2 tablespoons vegetable oil
2 tablespoons butter
1 large onion, finely chopped
1 clove garlic, crushed (optional)
3 tablespoons finely chopped fresh coriander (see Variation)
3 cups water
⅔ cup white wine
1 can (about 8 oz) tomatoes, drained and chopped
salt and freshly ground black pepper

1 Heat the oil and butter in a large heavy-based saucepan, add the onion, the garlic, if using, and the coriander and cook gently for about 5 minutes until the onion is soft and lightly colored.
2 Pour in the water and wine and add the tomatoes. Season to taste with salt and pepper.

Cook's Notes

TIME
Preparing and cooking the soup takes about 30 minutes. Allow extra time for preparing the mussels.

PREPARATION
Check that the mussels are fresh: Tap any open ones against a work surface and discard if they do not shut. Pull away any beards (pieces of seaweed) gripped between the shells of mussels. Scrub the mussels under cold running water, then scrape away the encrustations with a sharp knife. Soak the mussels in fresh cold water to cover for 2-3 hours, changing the water several times during this period.

BUYING GUIDE
Fresh mussels are available from October-March. Always buy them the day you are going to eat them. Look for closed mussels with unbroken shells. Frozen shelled mussels, which are available all year round, can be used instead.

VARIATION
Use parsley or chervil instead of coriander.

SERVING IDEAS
The mussels can be eaten with the fingers so provide napkins and a large dish to put the empty shells in.

● 255 calories per portion

3 Add the mussels and bring to a boil. Cover the pan, lower the heat and simmer gently for about 10 minutes or until the mussel shells have opened. Discard any mussels that do not open during cooking.
4 Spoon the mussels and soup into a warmed soup tureen or individual soup bowls and serve at once (see Serving ideas).

Fish and vegetable soup

SERVES 4

½ lb cod steaks, thawed if frozen, bones and skin removed and cut into ¾-inch pieces
1 tablespoon vegetable oil
1 small onion, chopped
2 potatoes, cut into ½-inch dice (see Buying guide)
2 carrots, cut into ½-inch dice
3 tablespoons all-purpose flour
1¼ cups warm milk
2½ cups warm chicken broth
1 bay leaf
salt and freshly ground black pepper
¼ cup shelled shrimp
½ bunch watercress, stalks removed, to garnish

1 Heat the oil in a large saucepan, add the onion, potatoes and carrots and cook over gentle heat, stirring, for 3 minutes. !
2 Sprinkle in the flour, stir for 1 minute, then remove from heat and gradually stir in the milk and broth.
3 Return the pan to the heat and bring to boil, stirring. Lower heat, add bay leaf and salt and pepper to taste. Simmer for 15 minutes.
4 Add the cod to the pan and simmer for a further 10 minutes.
5 Discard the bay leaf, stir the shrimp into the soup and heat through for 5 minutes. ✳ Taste and adjust seasoning, then pour into warmed individual soup bowls and garnish with the watercress. Serve the soup at once.

Cook's Notes

TIME
Preparation takes 20 minutes and cooking about 35 minutes.

FREEZING
Make the soup without adding the watercress. Cool quickly, then freeze in a plastic bag or rigid container for up to 3 months. Reheat from frozen, adding a little extra milk or broth if liked.

VARIATIONS
Any white fish may be used instead of cod.
Use 2 tablespoons chopped parsley or chopped chives instead of the watercress.
Swirl 1 tablespoon cream on top of each bowl just before serving.

WATCHPOINT
Do not allow the vegetables to brown, or the soup will be light brown instead of pale and creamy.

BUYING GUIDE
Choose floury potatoes such as Idaho. Waxy potatoes are not suitable for this soup, as they do not disintegrate so easily.

● 250 calories per portion

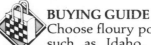

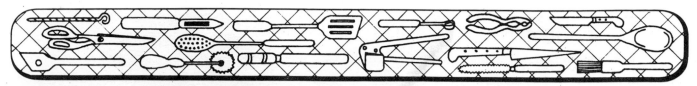

Corn and tuna chowder

 SERVES 4-6
1 can (about 12 oz) whole kernel corn
 1 can (about 7 oz) tuna
2 tablespoons butter or margarine
1 large onion, finely chopped
2 tablespoons all-purpose flour
2 teaspoons paprika
pinch of cayenne pepper
3¾ cups milk
pinch of salt
grated rind of ½ lemon

TO FINISH
½ cup finely grated Cheddar cheese
4 tablespoons chopped parsley

1 Drain the corn kernels, reserving the juice. Drain off the oil from the tuna fish and discard. Place the tuna on paper towels to remove excess oil. ☐ Flake all the tuna into a bowl.

2 Melt the butter in a saucepan, add the onion and cook gently until soft but not colored.
3 Stir in the flour, paprika and cayenne pepper and cook for 1 minute, stirring constantly with a wooden spoon. Gradually stir in 1½ cups milk and reserved corn juice and bring to a boil, stirring.
4 Stir in the remaining milk and bring the mixture to simmering point. Add the salt and the grated lemon rind.
5 Add the corn and then simmer the soup, uncovered, for 5 minutes. Add the tuna fish and simmer for a further 5 minutes until heated through.
6 To finish: Taste and adjust seasoning, then pour into warmed individual soup bowls. Sprinkle with the cheese ☐ and parsley and serve at once.

Cook's Notes

TIME
The soup takes 30 minutes to prepare and cook.

COOK'S TIP
To make the soup in advance, prepare it up to the end of stage 4, leave to cool, then refrigerate. To finish: Reheat until bubbling, stirring constantly, then continue from stage 5.

WATCHPOINT
It is important to remove as much oil as possible from the tuna so that the chowder is not greasy.
Always add the cheese just before serving, when the soup is still hot enough for it to melt. Do not bring back to a boil after adding the cheese or the soup will be stringy.

● 410 calories per portion

Provencal fish chowder

SERVES 4-6

1½ lb firm white fish fillets, skinned and cut into 1½-inch pieces (see Variation)
3 tablespoons vegetable oil
1 lb onions, grated
1 can (about 2 lb) tomatoes
bouquet garni
2 potatoes, cut into small ½-inch cubes
24 small black olives, halved and pitted
2 tablespoons capers, drained
1¼ cups tomato juice
2½ cups vegetable broth (see Preparation)
salt and freshly ground black pepper
3 tablespoons finely chopped fresh parsley

1 Heat the oil in a large saucepan, add the onions and cook gently for 5 minutes until soft and lightly colored. Add the tomatoes, with their juice, and the bouquet garni. Bring to a boil, then lower the heat and simmer for 5 minutes, stirring and breaking up the tomatoes with a wooden spoon.

2 Add all the remaining ingredients except the parsley and simmer un-covered, for 10-15 minutes, or until the potato is cooked (see Cook's tip).

3 Add the fish to the pan and simmer gently, uncovered, for about 5 minutes, or until the fish is tender but not breaking up. Remove the bouquet garni, stir in the parsley, then taste and adjust seasoning. Transfer to a warmed serving bowl and serve at once.

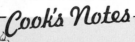

Cook's Notes

 TIME
Total preparation and cooking time is about 50 minutes.

 PREPARATION
For vegetable broth, save the liquid from cooked vegetables such as carrots and cabbage. Alternatively, use a vegetable bouillon cube, from health food shops.

SPECIAL OCCASION
This soup is a filling appetizer and can also make a lunch or supper party dish. Give it a real Mediterranean flavor by adding a crushed clove of garlic.

VARIATION
Use haddock fillets to make this a very special fish chowder.

 COOK'S TIP
You can prepare the chowder up to the end of stage 2 the day before, then add the fish and complete the cooking just before serving.

 SERVING IDEAS
Serve with toasted French bread and butter.

● 395 calories per portion

Pea soup with cheese toast

SERVES 4

1 large can (about 1lb 3oz) green peas
1 tablespoon dried onion flakes
2 tablespoons boiling water
1¼ cups chicken broth
½ teaspoon dried thyme
3 tablespoons instant potato powder (see Cook's tip)
1-2 teaspoons lemon juice
2-3 tablespoons evaporated milk or light cream
salt and freshly ground black pepper
1 tablespoon finely chopped fresh parsley

TOAST

4 small thick slices whole wheat bread
½ cup grated Cheddar cheese
2 tablespoons evaporated milk
¼ teaspoon prepared English mustard

1 Put the dried onion flakes into a cup, pour over the boiling water and leave to stand for at least 15 minutes.
2 Put the peas with their liquid in the pitcher of a blender with the onion mixture and blend until smooth. Work through a strainer. Put into a saucepan with the broth and thyme and bring to a boil over moderate heat.
3 Lower the heat and sprinkle in the potato powder. Stir for 1-2 minutes then remove from heat and stir in the lemon juice and milk. Season to taste with salt and pepper. Return to the heat and simmer gently while you prepare the toast.
4 Preheat the broiler to high, and toast the bread on both sides. Remove from the broiler.
5 Mix the cheese with the milk, mustard and salt and pepper.
6 Spread the cheese mixture on the toast, return to the broiler and cook until the cheese mixture browns.
7 Ladle the soup into warmed individual bowls. Cut each slice of toast into 4 and top with parsley.

Celery and peanut soup

SERVES 4

4 large celery stalks, chopped (see Economy)

6 tablespoons crunchy peanut butter

1 tablespoon butter or margarine

1 tablespoon vegetable oil

1 onion, chopped

3 cups light broth

salt and freshly ground black pepper

4 tablespoons light cream, to serve

chopped celery leaves, to garnish

1 Heat the butter and oil in a saucepan, add the celery and onion and cook gently for 5 minutes until the onion is soft and lightly colored.

2 Add the broth and bring to a boil. Lower the heat, cover and simmer gently for about 30 minutes until the celery is tender.

3 Cool the mixture a little, then work in a blender for a few seconds until smooth.

4 Return to the rinsed-out pan, place over low heat, then beat in the peanut butter. Heat through until just boiling. ✳ Taste and then adjust seasoning.

5 Ladle the soup into 4 warmed individual bowls. Stir 1 tablespoon cream into each, then wait for a few seconds for the cream to rise to the surface. Sprinkle the chopped celery leaves in the center of the bowls and serve at once.

Cook's Notes

TIME
Total preparation and cooking time is about 45 minutes.

FREEZING
Cool quickly, then pour into a rigid container, leaving ¾-inch headspace. Seal, label and freeze for up to 2 months. To serve: Thaw at room temperature for 2 hours, then reheat in a heavy-based pan, stirring frequently until bubbling. Taste and adjust seasoning, then proceed from the beginning of stage 5.

ECONOMY
This is a good way of using up outside celery stalks which may be a little tough, saving the more tender inner stalks for use in salads or serving with cheese.

SERVING IDEAS
Serve with freshly baked bread or rolls – white or whole wheat rolls or those coated with a sprinkling of sesame or poppy seeds go particularly well with this soup.

● 265 calories per portion

Cheesy potato soup

SERVES 4

1½ lb potatoes, pared and cut into even-sized pieces

salt

2 tablespoons butter or margarine

1 large onion, finely chopped

2 large cloves garlic, finely chopped (optional)

3 celery stalks, finely chopped

1 large carrot, diced small

¼ small rutabaga (weighing about ⅛ lb), diced small

1¼ cup chicken or vegetable broth (see Cook's tip)

⅔ cup milk

½ teaspoon dried thyme or marjoram

½ teaspoon celery salt

freshly ground black pepper

¾ cup grated Cheddar cheese

3 tablespoons chopped parsley

1 Cook the potatoes in enough boiling salted water to cover for about 15 minutes or until tender.

2 When the potatoes are cooked, leave them to cool slightly in the water, then transfer both potatoes and water to a blender and blend until smooth. (If you do not have a blender, pass them through a sieve.) Return the purée to the rinsed-out pan.

3 Melt the butter in a large skillet, add the onion and garlic, if using, and cook over moderate heat until beginning to soften. Add the remaining vegetables to the pan and cook, stirring occasionally, for about 10 minutes, until just beginning to color.

4 Mix the vegetables with the potato purée in the saucepan, then stir in the broth, milk, thyme and celery salt. Add pepper to taste.

5 Bring to a boil, lower the heat and simmer gently for about 15 minutes or until the vegetables are just soft. [!] Stir in the cheese, reserving 2 tablespoons, and simmer for a further 2-3 minutes. Taste and adjust seasoning.

6 Pour into a warmed soup tureen. Sprinkle with the chopped parsley and the remaining cheese and serve at once.

Leek and barley soup

SERVES 4

 4 leeks, sliced
¼ cup pearl barley
 1 tablespoon vegetable oil
1 small onion, chopped
2 carrots, sliced
1 can (about 14 oz) tomatoes
2½ cups vegetable broth or water
　(see Cook's tip)
½ teaspoon dried mixed herbs
1 bay leaf
salt and freshly ground black pepper
1 can (about 7 oz) butter or lima
　beans, drained

CHEESY BREAD
4 round slices French bread, ¾-inch
　thick
3 tablespoons butter, for cooking
1 clove garlic, cut in half (optional)
1 cup grated Cheddar cheese

1 Heat the oil in a large saucepan, add the onion, leeks and carrots and cook gently for 3-4 minutes.
2 Add the tomatoes with their juice, the broth and the barley, herbs and bay leaf. Season to taste with salt and pepper. Bring to a boil, stirring, then lower the heat, cover and simmer for 50 minutes. Stir occasionally during this time. ✳
3 Meanwhile, make the cheesy bread: Melt the butter in a skillet and when it sizzles add the slices of French bread. Cook over fairly high heat, turning once, until the bread is crisp and golden brown on both sides. Remove from the pan, drain on paper towels and leave to cool.
4 Rub each side of fried bread with the cut sides of the garlic, if using. Press the grated cheese evenly onto the slices of bread, dividing it equally between them. Preheat the broiler to high.
5 Remove the bay leaf from the soup, stir in the drained beans and heat through. Adjust seasoning.

Cook's Notes

TIME
Preparation takes 15 minutes, cooking 1 hour.

COOK'S TIP
Vegetable bouillon cubes are difficult to obtain, but you may find them in a good specialty food stores. To make your own vegetable broth, simply use the liquid in which you have cooked vegetables.

FREEZING
Cool the soup quickly after stage 2, discard the bay leaf, then freeze in a rigid container for up to 3 months. To thaw: Place the soup in a large saucepan and cook over low heat, stirring from time to time. Make the cheesy bread and add the beans as from the beginning of stage 3.

● 340 calories per portion

6 Toast the cheese-topped slices of bread until the cheese starts to bubble.
7 Ladle the soup into 4 warmed individual soup bowls and top each one with a slice of cheesy bread. Serve at once.

Chilled zucchini and cheese soup

SERVES 6

1 lb zucchini, cut into 1-inch lengths
3¾ cups chicken broth
1 mint sprig
2 tablespoons butter or margarine
1 onion, chopped
1 clove garlic, crushed (optional)
⅓ lb cream or Boursin cheese (see Economy)
⅔ cup milk
salt and freshly ground black pepper

TO SERVE

6 ice cubes
2 tablespoons heavy cream (see Economy)
extra mint sprigs, to garnish

1 Put the zucchini into a large pan with the broth and mint sprig. Bring to a boil, then lower the heat and simmer for 10 minutes.

2 Meanwhile, melt the butter in a small pan, add the onion and garlic, if using, and cook gently for 5 minutes until the onion is soft and lightly colored.

3 Remove the zucchini from the heat and stir in the onion and garlic. Allow to cool slightly, then pour the zucchini mixture into a blender and work to a purée.

4 In a large bowl, blend the cheese with the milk a little at a time, then beat with a wooden spoon until smooth and creamy. Stir in the zucchini purée.

5 Pour the soup into a clean large bowl or soup tureen, cover and refrigerate for about 4 hours or overnight.

6 To serve: Season the soup to taste with salt and pepper (see Cook's tip). Add ice cubes, swirl over the cream and sprinkle with sprigs of mint. Serve at once.

Cook's Notes

 TIME
15 minutes preparation, cooking time 10 minutes, then chill for 4 hours or overnight.

 VARIATION
Instead of zucchini, use 1 large cucumber cut into ¾-inch lengths.

 ECONOMY
For a less expensive soup lower in calories, use a curd cheese instead of full-fat cheese and plain yoghurt instead of the heavy cream.

COOK'S TIP
Wait until the soup has chilled and the flavors have developed before adding the seasoning.

SERVING IDEAS
Served just with fresh rolls or crusty bread and butter, this soup makes a delicious lunch for a hot day.

● 180 calories per portion

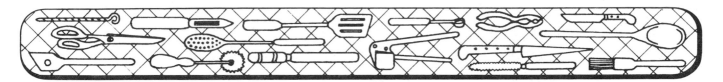

Chilled carrot and orange soup

SERVES 4

1 lb carrots, thinly sliced
1 tablespoon vegetable oil
1 onion, finely chopped
2 tablespoons medium-dry sherry
  (optional)
2½ cups chicken broth
salt and freshly ground black pepper
grated rind of 1 orange
juice of 3 large oranges
1 small carrot, grated, to garnish

1 Heat the oil in a saucepan, add the onion and cook gently for 5 minutes until soft and lightly colored. Add the sherry, if using, and bring to a boil

2 Add the sliced carrots and broth to the pan and season to taste.

3 Bring to a boil, stirring, then lower the heat, cover and simmer gently for 45 minutes until the carrots are very tender. Leave to cool.

4 Pass the soup through a strainer or purée in a blender. Pour the soup into a bowl, cover and refrigerate

Cook's Notes

TIME
15 minutes preparation, 45 minutes cooking, plus 2 hours chilling time.

VARIATION
¼ cup unsweetened concentrated orange juice may be substituted for the fresh orange juice.

SERVING IDEAS
If serving the soup at a summer dinner party,

give it a special garnish. Cut half an orange into 4 very thin slices. Remove the rind and pith. Float 1 orange slice on top of each bowl of chilled soup and arrange a little grated carrot on top of the slices.

The soup can also be served hot: Prepare to stage 3 but do not cool, reduce to a purée at once and reheat gently with the orange rind and juice.

● 130 calories per portion

for at least 2 hours or overnight.
5 Just before serving, stir the orange rind and juice into the soup, then taste and adjust seasoning. Pour into 4 chilled individual soup bowls, sprinkle a little grated carrot onto each bowl and serve at once.

PATES AND MOUSSES

Mixed fish pâté

SERVES 4
1 can (about 6 oz) tuna fish in oil
1 can (about 4½ oz) mackerel fillets
   in oil
¼ cup butter, melted and cooled
grated rind of 1 lemon
1 tablespoon lemon juice
1 clove garlic, crushed (optional)
salt and freshly ground black pepper
1 tablespoon light cream (optional)

TO GARNISH
few lemon slices
1-2 parsley sprigs

1 Place the tuna and mackerel, with
their oil, in a blender or food
processor. Pour over the melted
butter and add the lemon rind and
juice and the garlic, if using.
2 Blend to a smooth purée. Season
well and stir in the cream, if using.
3 Spoon into individual dishes,
cover and refrigerate for 2 hours.
4 Garnish with lemon slices and
parsley. Served chilled with toast.

Cook's Notes

TIME
10 minutes preparation,
plus 2 hours chilling.

COOK'S TIPS
The beauty of this paté
is that it can be made in
superquick time, from pantry-
shelf ingredients. This makes it
ideal for an impromptu appetizer or snack.

VARIATION
Large supermarkets
stock cans of tuna with
vegetables in a curry sauce. If
this is used instead of plain tuna
in oil, it will make the paté more
exotic, with just a hint of curry.

● 270 calories per portion

22

Quick sardine pâté

SERVES 4

1 can (about 15 oz) sardines in tomato sauce (see Cook's tip)
3 tablespoons heavy cream
½ teaspoon Worcestershire sauce
few drops of hot-pepper sauce
2 teaspoons lemon juice
2 tablespoons finely chopped dill pickles
salt and freshly ground black pepper

TO GARNISH
1 tablespoon chopped fresh parsley or flat-leaved parsley sprigs
4 dill pickle fans

1 Drain the sardines and reserve 1 tablespoon of the tomato sauce. Cut the sardines in half.

2 Place the fish in a bowl with the reserved tomato sauce, the cream, Worcestershire sauce, pepper-sauce, lemon juice and pickles. Beat together thoroughly with a fork and season to taste with salt and pepper.

3 Spoon the mixture into a serving bowl or 4 individual bowls, cover with plastic wrap and then refrigerate for 30 minutes.

4 To serve: Garnish the sardine paté with finely chopped parsley or parsley sprigs and the prepared pickle fans and serve chilled (see Serving ideas).

Egg pâté

SERVES 4

½ lb cream cheese
4 hard-boiled eggs, shelled and
   roughly chopped (see Cook's tip)
1 tablespoon finely chopped chives
salt and freshly ground black pepper
stuffed olives, sliced, to garnish

1 Put the cheese into a bowl and beat until soft. Beat in the chopped eggs and chives and season well with salt and pepper.
2 Spoon into 4 individual dishes. Smooth the top of each with a round-bladed knife, cover with plastic wrap and refrigerate for 30 minutes.
3 To serve: Garnish with the olive slices and serve at once.

Cook's Notes

TIME
Preparation (including hard-boiling the eggs) takes about 30 minutes, but allow another 30 minutes for chilling.

VARIATIONS
Use a full-fat soft cheese flavored with chives, herbs, garlic or crushed peppercorns, and omit the chives and/or the black pepper. For an extra "tangy" flavor, add 1 teaspoon good mustard or Worcestershire sauce or a dash of hot-pepper sauce.

COOK'S TIP
Hard-boiled eggs can be kept, unshelled, in a plastic bag in the refrigerator for 3-4 days.

SERVING IDEAS
Serve as a dinner party appetizer or snack with toast fingers or bread rolls.

● 305 calories per portion

Vegetable terrine

SERVES 4

12 cabbage leaves (see Buying guide), central midribs removed
salt
1 carrot (about ¼ lb), cut into matchstick lengths
1 zucchini (about ¼ lb), cut into matchstick lengths
1 can (about 7 oz) **corn and pimiento,** drained
2 eggs, plus 1 egg yolk
⅔ cup milk
3 tablespoons heavy cream
¼ teaspoon ground nutmeg
freshly ground black pepper
vegetable oil, for brushing

TOMATO SAUCE
½ lb tomatoes, roughly chopped
3 tablespoons plain yoghurt
1 teaspoon Dijon-style mustard
1 teaspoon Worcestershire sauce
1 teaspoon tomato catsup
pinch of sugar

1 Preheat the oven to 325°.
2 Bring a saucepan of salted water to a boil and blanch the cabbage leaves for 2 minutes. Drain and dry on a clean dish towel.
3 Bring a saucepan of salted water to a boil and put the carrot and zucchini matchsticks in to simmer for 5 minutes. Drain and refresh under cold water, drain again.
4 Brush a 8½ × 4½ × 2½ inch loaf pan with oil. Line the loaf pan with 3 or 4 of the largest cabbage leaves and chop the remainder fairly finely.
5 Put half the carrot and zucchini mixture into the lined loaf pan, add about half the corn and pimiento, then half the chopped cabbage. Repeat the layering to make 6 layers in all.
6 Beat the eggs lightly with the extra yolk, milk, cream and nutmeg. Season with salt and pepper. Carefully pour the egg mixture into the loaf pan, gently easing the vegetables apart in several places with a round-bladed knife, to make sure the egg mixture is evenly distributed through the pan and goes right to the bottom. Fold any protruding cabbage leaves over the

filling. Cover the pan with foil.
7 Set the loaf pan in a roasting pan. Pour in hot water to come three-quarters up the sides of the loaf pan and cook for 1½-2 hours, until the custard is set and firm to the touch. Remove the loaf pan from the roasting pan and cool. Chill overnight in the refrigerator.
8 To make the sauce: Put the tomatoes in a blender for a few seconds until liquidized, then strain to remove the skins and seeds.

9 Mix the tomato purée with the remaining sauce ingredients, stirring to make sure they are well combined. Season to taste with salt and pepper. Cover with plastic wrap and chill for at least 2 hours.
10 To serve: Allow the terrine to stand at room temperature for about 10 minutes. Run a knife around the sides of the terrine, invert a serving plate on top and shake gently to unmold. Serve cut in slices (see Cook's tips) with the tomato sauce.

Three-tier pâté

SERVES 4

 ½ lb liver sausage
5 tablespoons butter, softened
 ¼ cup blanched almonds, finely
chopped
a few black peppercorns, finely
crushed
1 teaspoon medium sherry
salt
1 cup grated Cheddar cheese
2 teaspoons chopped chives
2 teaspoons finely chopped fresh
parsley
1 cup cream cheese
2 teaspoons tomato paste
good pinch of paprika

1 Line the base of a freezerproof rigid container, which is approximately 4 inches square and 3 inches deep, with foil or alternatively waxed paper.

2 Using 1 tablespoon of the butter, thoroughly grease the base and sides of the container, then coat with the chopped almonds.

3 Mix together the liver sausage, black peppercorns, sherry and salt to taste. Spoon this mixture into the prepared container and press down firmly. Smooth the surface with a wet round-bladed knife.

4 In a bowl, beat together the remaining butter, the Cheddar cheese, chives, parsley and salt to taste. Spread this mixture over the liver sausage.

5 Beat the cream cheese in a separate bowl with the tomato paste, paprika and salt to taste. Spoon into the container and spread evenly on top of the Cheddar cheese mixture.

6 Cover and refrigerate for 1-2 hours.

7 To serve: Carefully run a knife around the sides of the container, then invert a serving plate on top. Invert the container onto the plate, remove the container and foil.

Meat terrine

SERVES 6

½ lb chicken livers
½ lb boneless fresh bacon with some fat
1 small onion, cut into chunks
½ lb ground beef
1 tablespoon tomato paste
½ teaspoon dried oregano
1 clove garlic, crushed (optional)
3 tablespoons red wine (see Economy)
salt and freshly ground black pepper
¼ lb stuffed olives
3 bay leaves
1 tablespoon chopped parsley, to garnish

1 Preheat the oven to 350°.
2 Wash and trim the livers, removing any discolored parts with a sharp knife.
3 Mince the livers, pork and onion finely in a mincer or chop finely in a food processor (see Cook's tip). Place in a large bowl and stir in the ground beef, tomato paste, oregano, garlic, if using, and wine. Mix thoroughly and season generously with salt and pepper.
4 Reserve 3 of the olives for garnish, then halve the rest. Spoon half of the terrine mixture into a 9 × 5 × 3 inch loaf pan or dish. Arrange the halved olives in the dish (see Preparation).
5 Carefully spoon the remaining terrine mixture on top of the olives and arrange the bay leaves on top. Tap the base of dish a few times on a work surface so the mixture fills the gaps between the olives. Cover the dish loosely with foil.
6 Put the dish into a roasting pan, pour in boiling water to come halfway up the sides of the dish and cook in the oven for about 1½ hours. To test for doneness, tilt the dish and if the juices run clear the terrine is cooked. Remove the dish from the roasting pan and cover the surface of the terrine with foil. Put heavy weights on top, leave to cool, then refrigerate overnight.
7 To serve: Turn the terrine out onto a platter. Slice the reserved olives and arrange them down the center of the terrine. Sprinkle a row of chopped parsley either side.

Cook's Notes

 TIME
The terrine takes about 20 minutes to prepare, plus 1½ hours cooking time; it then needs to be left overnight in the refrigerator.

 COOK's TIP
When mincing meats or fish, put a piece of bread into the mincer at the end as it helps to push out the last of the ingredients and their juices.

PREPARATION
To make a decorative effect:

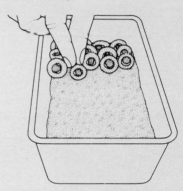

Arrange the halved olives sideways in rows across the terrine so that the cut sides face one of the ends of the dish and will be seen when the terrine is cut.

 VARIATION
Use ¼ lb sliced mushrooms instead of the olives. Cook them for 2 minutes in 2 tablespoons butter before using.

 SERVING IDEAS
Serve as an appetizer spread on thin slices of hot toast or alternatively serve with crusty bread and a fresh green salad for a tasty supper.

 ECONOMY
Serve the remaining wine with the terrine, or to be more economical, buy a small bottle of cooking wine concentrate. These are now widely available in supermarkets and liquor stores.

● 335 calories per portion

Pâté puffs

SERVES 4
¼ lb smoked bacon slices, rinds
  removed and finely diced
1 tablespoon butter or margarine
¾ cup finely chopped mushrooms
  (about 2 oz)
1 tablespoon chopped fresh parsley
celery or garlic salt (optional)
freshly ground black pepper
1 sheet (½ of 17 oz package) frozen
  puff pastry, thawed
¼ lb liver pâté (see Buying
  guide)
1 egg, beaten
1-2 tablespoons sesame seeds

TO GARNISH (optional)
lettuce
tomato slices

1 Melt the butter in a skillet over
moderate heat, add the bacon and
cook for 2-3 minutes. Add the
mushrooms and cook for about 5
minutes. Stir in the parsley and
season to taste with celery salt, if
using, and pepper. ⚠ Set aside to
cool slightly.
2 Preheat the oven to 400°.
3 Roll out the puff pastry on
a floured surface to a square
measuring about 12 inches. Trim
the edges to straighten them, then
cut it into 16 squares about 3 inches
each.
4 Mash the pâté with a fork to
soften it then divide it between the
16 squares spreading it roughly in
the center of each one. Top with the
bacon and mushroom mixture.
5 Brush the beaten egg around the
edges of each pastry square. Carefully fold over the pastry to make a
triangle, keeping the filling away
from the edges. Press the edges of
the pastry together firmly to seal
them. ⚠ Brush with beaten egg.
6 Put the triangles on a large
dampened cookie sheet and sprinkle
over the sesame seeds.
7 Bake for about 10-15 minutes
until the pastry is puffy and golden.
Lift the puffs off the cookie sheet at
once and cool slightly on a wire
rack. Arrange the hot puffs on a
plate garnished with lettuce and
tomato, if using.

Chicken liver and walnut pâté

SERVES 12
1 lb chicken livers
¼ lb walnuts or pecans, chopped
¼ lb butter
1 small onion, finely chopped
1-2 cloves garlic, crushed (optional)
2 bay leaves
¼ lb bacon slices
2 tablespoons dry or medium sherry
1 tablespoon brandy
2 large eggs, beaten
pinch of freshly ground nutmeg
salt and freshly ground black
   pepper

1 Melt the butter in a saucepan, add the chicken livers, onion, garlic, if using, bay leaves and bacon. Simmer gently for 10 minutes, stirring from time to time. Remove from the heat and leave to cool for about 30 minutes.
2 Preheat the oven to 325°.
3 Remove the bay leaves from the liver mixture and put the mixture through a mincer or chop finely. Stir in the remaining ingredients with salt and pepper to taste. Mix thoroughly.
4 Transfer the mixture to a 7-inch terrine or loaf pan or a 1-quart round or oval ovenproof dish.
5 Place the dish in a roasting pan and pour in enough water to come halfway up the dish. Bake in the oven for 1½ hours or until firm to the touch. Leave until cold then cover and refrigerate overnight.
6 Serve straight from the dish, or run a knife around the edge of the dish, then invert a serving plate on top of the dish. Hold the mold and plate firmly together and invert them giving a sharp shake halfway around. Serve cut into slices.

Quick tuna pâté

SERVES 4

1 can (about 7 oz) tuna, drained and flaked
4 tablespoons thick mayonnaise
4 tablespoons butter, melted
few drops of hot-pepper sauce
2 teaspoons lemon juice
2 teaspoons capers, drained and chopped
salt and freshly ground black pepper
4 black olives, pitted and sliced (optional)
4 tablespoons consommé (see Cook's tip)

1 Mix the tuna, mayonnaise, butter, pepper sauce and lemon juice in a bowl until well blended. Stir in the capers and season the mixture

with both salt and pepper to taste.
2 Spoon the mixture into 4 individual serving dishes. Smooth the surfaces and arrange the olive slices on top, if using.

3 Gently heat the consommé in a saucepan and spoon 1 tablespoon over each paté. Refrigerate for 10 minutes, until the consommé has set (see Serving ideas).

Cook's Notes

 TIME
This pâté takes only 10 minutes to prepare, plus 10 minutes chilling time in the refrigerator.

 SERVING IDEAS
This quickly made paté is ideal for impromptu entertaining: Made from pantry-shelf ingredients, it is really a useful recipe to remember for unexpected guests. Serve with hot whole wheat or granary toast and butter for an appetizer, or with French bread and a mixed salad for a light lunch.

 VARIATION
Use canned red salmon, drained and flaked, instead of the tuna.

 COOK'S TIP
Consommé, which is a useful pantry-shelf item, is available in cans of about 10 oz. Left-over consummé can be kept in refrigerator 4-5 days, dice and add to chilled soups or dilute with water and use as broth in sauces and casseroles.

● 285 calories per portion

Quick pâté mousse

SERVES 4-6

2 cans (about 7 oz each) pork or
    chicken paté
⅓ lb cream cheese with
    chives
3 tablespoons chopped chives
2-3 tablespoons brandy
freshly ground black pepper
few stuffed olives and small dill
    pickles, to garnish

1 Put all the ingredients, except the garnish, in a blender or food processor and work for several minutes until smooth (see Cook's tip).
2 Spoon the mixture into individual serving bowls, or 1 large bowl.
3 Cover and refrigerate for several hours or overnight.
4 Remove from the refrigerator 30 minutes before serving to allow to come to room temperature. Garnish with stuffed olives and pickles.

Cook's Notes

 TIME
The preparation only takes 10 minutes, but allow several hours chilling time.

COOK'S TIP
If you do not have a blender or food processor, mash the ingredients together with a fork. Add a little cream if you find that the mixture is very stiff.

 VARIATIONS
Substitute fresh herbs of your choice instead of the chives. Whisky or an orange-flavored liqueur may be used instead of the brandy. Decorate with black olives instead of stuffed olives.

SERVING IDEAS
Serve with hot toast or crisp crackers as an appetizer or lunchtime or evening snack, or as part of a cold buffet.

● 520 calories per portion

Salmon mousse

SERVES 4-6

1 can (about 7 oz) salmon, drained,
    with juice reserved
about 1 cup milk
2 tablespoons butter or margarine
4 tablespoons all-purpose
    flour
2 eggs, separated
2 envelopes unflavored gelatin
2 tablespoons lemon juice
2 tablespoons water
2 tablespoons tomato catsup
⅔ cup light cream
salt and freshly ground black pepper
sprigs of dill
cucumber slices, to garnish

1 Strain the juice from the salmon
into a measuring jug and make up to
1¼ cups with milk.
2 Melt the butter in a small
saucepan, sprinkle in the flour and
stir over low heat for 1-2 minutes

until straw-colored. Remove from
the heat and gradually stir in the
milk mixture. Return to the heat and
simmer, stirring, until thick and
smooth.
3 Remove from the heat and stir in
the egg yolks.
4 Mash the fish roughly with a fork,
discarding all skin and bones. Stir
into the sauce, then work the
mixture in a blender for a few
seconds until smooth. Pour into a
clean bowl and set aside to cool.
5 Sprinkle the gelatin over the
lemon juice and water in a small
flameproof bowl. Leave to soak for
5 minutes until spongy then stand
the bowl in a pan of gently
simmering water for 1-2 minutes,
stirring occasionally, until the gelatin has dissolved.
6 Remove from the heat, leave to
cool slightly, then stir into the
salmon mixture with the tomato
catsup and cream. Season to taste
with salt and pepper. Cover and
refrigerate for 2-3 hours, or until on
the point of setting.
7 In a clean, dry bowl, beat the

Cook's Notes

TIME
Preparation time is
about 30 minutes, but
allow overnight refrigeration.

VARIATION
Omit dill sprigs and
set in a soufflé dish.
Do not turn out, but garnish the
top of the mousse decoratively
with thin cucumber and lemon
slices, if wished.

●320 calories per portion

egg whites until standing in stiff
peaks, then fold into salmon mixture
with a large metal spoon.
8 Line base of an oiled 3-cup tube
pan with dill sprigs. Spoon salmon
mixture carefully on top. Refrigerate overnight.
9 Dip base of pan in hot water for
10 seconds, then turn mousse out
onto a serving plate. Serve chilled,
garnished with cucumber.

Egg and cucumber mousse

SERVES 6

4 hard-boiled eggs, shelled and
   chopped
½ lb cucumber, quartered
   lengthwise
1 teaspoon salt
3 large scallions
   (including green tops), finely
   chopped
4 tablespoons chopped fresh
   parsley
2 teaspoons unflavored gelatin
3 tablespoons water
⅔ cup thick mayonnaise
⅓ cup plain yogurt
freshly ground black pepper
1 egg white

1 Scrape out the cucumber seeds
with a teaspoon and chop the
cucumber finely. Spread it out on a
plate and sprinkle with salt. Put
another plate over the cucumber

and place heavy weights on top.
Leave for 30 minutes, then drain
thoroughly.
2 Put the hard-boiled eggs, cucumber, onions and parsley into a bowl
and mix well.
3 Sprinkle the gelatin over the
water in a small flameproof bowl
and leave to soak for 5 minutes, until
spongy. Stand the bowl in a pan of
gently simmering water and leave
for 1-2 minutes, stirring occasionally, until gelatin has dissolved.
4 In a large bowl, blend the
mayonnaise with the yogurt.
Allow the gelatin liquid to cool
slightly, then stir it briskly into the
mayonnaise mixture. Stir in the egg
mixture and pepper to taste. Cover
and refrigerate for 30-40 minutes,
until beginning to set.
5 In a clean dry bowl, beat the egg
white until standing in stiff peaks,
then fold it into the egg mixture
with a large metal spoon. Turn the
mousse into a 4-cup serving dish,
cover and refrigerate for about 2
hours, until set. Serve chilled (see
Serving ideas).

Cook's Notes

 TIME
30 minutes draining for
the cucumber, then 30
minutes preparation, plus about
2 hours setting time.

 SERVING IDEAS
Garnish the mousse
with slices of hard-
boiled egg and drained canned
anchovy fillets. (To reduce
saltiness, soak the fillets in milk
for 20 minutes, then drain and
pat dry.) Serve as an appetizer
or snack with Melba toast.

 VARIATION
For an egg and sweet
pepper mousse, omit
the cucumber and parsley; seed
and dice 1 small red and 1 small
yellow pepper and add to the
chopped egg and onions. Garnish with strips of pepper.

● 230 calories per portion

Zucchini and tomato mousse

SERVES 4-6

½ lb zucchini, sliced about
  ½-inch thick
2 tablespoons butter or margarine
⅔ cup thick mayonnaise
⅔ cup cold chicken broth
2 eggs, separated
3 tablespoons water
4 teaspoons unflavored gelatin
2 tablespoons chopped chives
few drops hot-pepper sauce
  (optional)
salt and freshly ground black pepper
½ lb tomatoes, peeled,
  seeded and diced
  (see Cook's tip)

TO GARNISH
tomato slices
1 tablespoon chopped chives

1 Melt the butter in a large skillet over low heat, add the zucchini and cook gently for about 15 minutes until soft, stirring so that the zucchini do not brown.
2 Place the zucchini with the mayonnaise, chicken broth and egg yolks in a blender or food processor and blend to a purée.
3 Put the water in a bowl, sprinkle over the gelatin and leave to soak until spongy. Then stand the bowl in a pan of hot water and stir until the gelatin is dissolved and the liquid is clear.
4 Turn the purée into a large bowl and stir in the chives and the pepper sauce, if using. Taste and season. Then stir in the dissolved gelatin. Leave in the refrigerator for about 30 minutes until just setting.
5 Stir the purée until smooth then stir in the diced tomato. Beat the egg whites until they stand in stiff peaks and then carefully fold into the purée.

6 Turn the mixture into a 5-cup soufflé dish and chill for about 1½ hours or until set.
7 Serve garnished with tomato slices and chopped chives.

FISH AND SEAFOOD

Fish gratin

SERVES 4

4 frozen cod steaks, total weight
    about 1 lb
⅔ cup water
1 small onion, sliced
1 bay leaf
salt and freshly ground black pepper
3 tablespoons butter or margarine
2 tablespoons all-purpose flour
⅔ cup milk
1 cup grated Cheddar cheese
1 cup fresh white bread crumbs
butter, for greasing

1 Grease 4 scallop shells or individual ovenproof dishes.

2 Put the frozen fish steaks into a heavy-based skillet. Pour over the water, then add the onion and bay leaf and season to taste with salt and pepper. Bring to a boil, then lower the heat, cover and simmer for 15 minutes.

3 With a slotted spatula, lift the fish and onion from the liquid. Strain the liquid and reserve.

4 Leave the fish until cool enough to handle, then flake the flesh. Divide the fish between the prepared dishes and set aside.

5 Preheat the broiler to medium.

6 Melt 2 tablespoons of the butter in a small saucepan, sprinkle in the flour and stir over low heat for 1-2 minutes until straw-colored. Then remove from the heat and gradually stir in the reserved fish liquid and then the milk. Return to the heat and simmer, stirring, until thick and smooth. Remove from the heat and stir in half the grated cheese. Stir vigorously until the cheese has melted, then season to taste.

7 Spoon the cheese sauce over the fish in each shell, dividing it equally between them. Mix the bread crumbs with the remaining cheese and sprinkle over the sauce in each shell. Dot with rest of butter.

8 Broil until golden brown and heated through and serve at once.

Cook's Notes

 TIME
Preparing and cooking take 40 minutes.

 VARIATIONS
Any white fish fillets such as haddock or whiting may be used instead of the cod steaks. If using fresh fish, simmer 10 minutes.

 ● 330 calories per portion

SPECIAL OCCASION
Pipe a border of mashed potatoes, to which some beaten egg has been added, around the edge of each shell before broiling.

Instead of cod, use monkfish, which tastes rather like lobster, and then add ¼ lb cooked shrimp in stage 4.

Replace the water with white wine.

Spicy fish

SERVES 4

¾ lb flounder or tilefish, bones
   removed, cut into 4 × ½-inch
   strips
   (see Buying guide)
1½ cups fresh white bread crumbs
½ cup shredded coconut
¼ teaspoon chili powder
½ teaspoon ground coriander
½ teaspoon ground cumin
salt and freshly ground black
   pepper
3 tablespoons all-purpose flour
2 eggs, beaten
¼ cucumber, pared and chopped
2 tablespoons chopped dill pickles
⅓ cup thick mayonnaise
vegetable oil, for deep-frying
lemon and tomato, to garnish

1 Put the bread crumbs in a bowl
and stir in the coconut, chili,
coriander and cumin. Season with
salt and black pepper to taste.

2 Spread the flour out on a large flat
plate and season with salt and
pepper. Beat the eggs in a shallow
bowl. Dip the fish strips in the flour,
turning to coat thoroughly, then in
the egg, and then in the bread crumb
mixture until evenly coated.

3 Lay the strips on a cookie sheet or
tray and refrigerate for 10 minutes.

4 Meanwhile, mix the cucumber
and pickles into the mayonnaise and
spoon into a small serving jug.
Preheat the oven to 225°.

5 Pour enough oil into a deep-fat
fryer with a basket to come halfway
up the sides. Heat the oil to 375°, or
until a stale bread cube turns golden
in 50 seconds. Fry the fish strips a
few at a time [!] for 5-7 minutes
until they are golden brown and
crisp.

6 Drain on paper towels and keep
warm in oven while frying remaining batches. Serve the fish strips at
once garnished with thin wedges of
lemon and tomato halves and with
the cucumber and pickle sauce
handed separately.

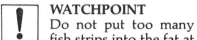

Dressed smoked mackerel

SERVES 4

1 lb smoked mackerel fillets, cut in half lengthwise if large (see Buying guide)
¼ cup thick mayonnaise, (preferably homemade)
2 tablespoons plain yogurt
¼ teaspoon Dijon-style mustard
salt and freshly ground black pepper
3 celery stalks, chopped
¾ cup green grapes, halved and pitted
¼ lb radishes, thinly sliced
4 large lettuce leaves

GARNISH
mustard and garden cress
1 lemon, cut into wedges

1 In a bowl, mix together the mayonnaise, yogurt and mustard and season to taste with salt and pepper. Stir in the celery, grapes and radishes.
2 Put the lettuce leaves on a serving dish. Arrange the mackerel fillets over them, slightly overlapping.
3 Spoon the salad mixture in a line on top of the mackerel. Garnish with the mustard and cress and lemon wedges.

Cook's Notes

 TIME
Preparation takes about 20 minutes.

 BUYING GUIDE
Ready-cooked whole smoked mackerel can be bought from good fishstores and delicatessens and are easily filleted. Frozen, vacuum-packed, or canned smoked mackerel fillets are available from supermarkets.

 SERVING IDEAS
For an even more substantial dish, serve with plain cooked rice to which some chopped nuts have been added.

● 425 calories per portion

Baked stuffed kippers

SERVES 4

4 kippered herrings, bones removed (see Preparation)
¼ cup butter or margarine
3 eggs, hard-boiled and chopped while hot
2 tablespoons chopped parsley
grated rind and juice of ½ lemon
freshly ground black pepper
12 slices lemon and a few small parsley sprigs, to garnish

1 Preheat the oven to 400°.
2 Cream the butter in a bowl with a wooden spoon and gradually work in the chopped eggs and parsley. Add the lemon rind and juice and season to taste with pepper. (Kippers can be salty so do not add salt.)
3 Cut 4 pieces of foil, each big enough to enclose a kipper.
4 Place a kipper on each piece of foil and spoon an equal amount of stuffing over the half of each kipper. Fold the kipper over the stuffing and wrap the foil into a loose parcel, turning in the ends of the foil to seal them tightly, so that the juices do not run out during cooking.
5 Place the parcels on a cookie sheet and cook in oven for 15-20 minutes.
6 Fold back the foil around the kippers, then carefully remove the skin from the top side, leaving on the heads and tails. Lay 3 lemon slices along each kipper and place a sprig of parsley in the center of each one.
7 Serve the kippers hot in the foil with their juices. If you prefer, use paper towels to drain away some of the juices first.

Cook's Notes

 TIME
Preparation 20 minutes (including boning the kippers), cooking 15-20 minutes.

 PREPARATION
Slide a sharp knife under the backbone and remove it with as many of the small bones as possible.

COOK'S TIP
If the kippers look dry, they can be made more succulent before cooking by placing them in a shallow dish and pouring over boiling water. Soak for 5 minutes, then dry thoroughly on paper towels.

 SERVING IDEAS
Chunks of French or granary bread are perfect for mopping up the kipper juices.

A tomato and cucumber salad provides a refreshing contrast to the rich flavor of kippers.

 VARIATIONS
Smoked mackerel can be substituted for the kippers. If kipper fillets are easier to obtain than whole kippers, use 2 per person and sandwich them together with the filling in between.

● 380 calories per portion

Creamy cod appetizer

SERVES 4

½ lb cod fillets, skinned
1¼ cups milk
2 tablespoons butter
2 tablespoons all-purpose flour
¼ lb frozen shelled shrimp thawed
2 tablespoons chopped fresh
   parsley

POTATO TOPPING
1¼ lb potatoes, cooked and
   mashed
2 tablespoons butter
2 tablespoons milk
pinch of freshly ground nutmeg
salt and freshly ground black pepper

TO GARNISH
shelled cooked shrimp
parsley sprigs

1 Pour the milk into a saucepan and heat until simmering. Add the cod and cover the pan. Simmer for 15 minutes or until the fish is cooked. Using a slotted spatula, transfer the cod to a plate, then flake the flesh with a fork, discarding any bones. Strain the broth into a jug and set aside.

2 Make the potato topping: Put the mashed potato in a bowl, then stir in the butter, milk [!] and nutmeg. Beat until smooth. Season to taste with salt and pepper, then spoon into a large pastry bag fitted with a medium-sized nozzle. Set aside.

3 Melt the butter in a saucepan, sprinkle in the flour and stir over low heat for 1-2 minutes until straw-colored. Remove from the heat and gradually stir in reserved broth. Return to the heat and simmer, stirring, until thick and smooth.

4 Stir in cod, shrimp and parsley. Simmer gently for 5 minutes and season with salt and pepper.

5 Preheat the broiler to high.

6 Divide the fish mixture equally between 4 small shallow flameproof pots or dishes. Pipe a border of potato around the edge of each pot, then put under the broiler for 3-4 minutes, until the potato border has browned a little.

7 Garnish each pot with a shrimp and a sprig of parsley. Serve at once.

Fish rolls

SERVES 4

2 flounder, divided into 8 fillets
¼ lb Cheddar cheese in 1 piece
2 large eggs, beaten
4 cups fresh white bread crumbs
vegetable oil, for deep frying

1 Skin and wash the fillets, then dry them on paper towels.
2 Cut the cheese into 8 pieces, each long enough to fit just across the width of a fish fillet. Place a piece of cheese on each fillet and roll it up, starting from the tail end.
3 Pour the beaten eggs onto a shallow dish and put the bread crumbs on a plate. Coat each fish roll all over in egg, then in bread crumbs. Repeat, so that the rolls are coated twice, pressing the second coating of bread crumbs on thoroughly.
4 Pour enough oil into a deep-fat fryer to cover the fish rolls and heat to 325° (see Cook's tips).

Carefully lower the fish rolls into the hot oil and cook for about 7 minutes until they are golden brown and crisp (fry the rolls in 2 batches if necessary). Remove with a spoon and drain on paper towels. Serve at once, with tartar sauce.

Cook's Notes

TIME
Preparation and cooking 30-45 minutes.

COOK'S TIPS
If you do not have a cooking thermometer or deep-fat fryer with its own thermostat, test the heat of the oil by dropping in a 1-inch cube of bread: this should brown in 75 seconds at a temperature of 325°.

 WATCHPOINT
It is very important to coat the rolls thoroughly in egg and bread crumbs, or the cheese will melt and it will bubble out.

● 510 calories per portion

Selsey soused herrings

SERVES 4

4 large herrings, each weighing about ½ lb, boned but left in 1 piece (see Buying guide)
salt and freshly ground black pepper
1 small onion, sliced
⅔ cup white wine vinegar
½ cup water
4 bay leaves
8 whole black peppercorns
1-inch stick cinnamon

TO SERVE

2 teaspoons creamed horseradish sauce
pinch of dry mustard
⅔ cup heavy cream
lemon and beet wedges, to garnish (optional)

1 Preheat the oven to 325°.
2 Season the herrings with salt and pepper and roll them up, starting from head end, with skin on outside and secure with toothpicks if necessary. Arrange them in a single layer in a casserole just large enough to hold them comfortably.
3 Add the onion, vinegar and water. Push the bay leaves, peppercorns and cinnamon between the herring rolls. Cover with a lid or foil and bake in the oven for 1 hour. Leave to cool in the cooking liquid for at least 8 hours.
4 Drain the herrings, reserving 4 tablespoons cooking liquid, and place on a serving dish.
5 Put the reserved liquid into a bowl with the horseradish sauce, mustard powder and cream and whisk until standing in soft peaks.
6 Spoon a little sauce over each herring and garnish with lemon and beet wedges, if liked. Serve cold, with the remaining cream sauce handed separately.

Cook's Notes

TIME
This recipe takes 10 minutes to prepare and 1 hour to cook, but allow a further 8 hours for cooling.

BUYING GUIDE
Ask your fishstore to bone the fish and cut off the head.

STORAGE
The flavor of soused herrings is best after they have been left for 24 hours, but they can be left in the refrigerator for up to 3-4 days.

SERVING IDEAS
Halve the herrings lengthwise before serving as an appetizer. Alternatively, for a complete meal, serve with potato salad and lettuce tossed in an oil and vinegar dressing.

DID YOU KNOW
This dish gets its name from Selsey in Sussex, England, and dates from a time when herrings were plentiful off England's south coast.

● 370 calories per portion

Salmon and macaroni layer

SERVES 4

1 can (about 7½ oz) salmon, drained
   with juice reserved, flaked
   (see Economy)
salt
1 cup elbow macaroni
2 tablespoons butter or margarine
2 tablespoons all-purpose flour
1¼ cups milk
2 hard-boiled eggs, chopped
1 tablespoon chopped fresh parsley
pinch of ground mace
freshly ground black pepper
¾ cup grated Cheddar cheese
tomato wedges and watercress,
   to garnish

1 Bring a large pan of salted water to a boil, add the macaroni and cook for 10 minutes until tender but firm to the bite (*al dente*).

2 Meanwhile, melt the butter in a saucepan, sprinkle in the flour and stir over low heat for 1-2 minutes until straw-colored. Remove from the heat and gradually stir in the milk and reserved salmon juice. Return to the heat and simmer, stirring, until thick and smooth.

3 Remove the sauce from the heat and gently fold in the eggs and salmon with the parsley and mace. Season to taste with salt and pepper, then spoon into a flameproof dish (see Serving ideas).

4 Drain the macaroni thoroughly and turn into a bowl. Add half the cheese and toss to coat well. Spoon the macaroni over the salmon mixture. Sprinkle over the remaining cheese. Broil for 5 minutes until the cheese is golden and bubbling. Garnish with tomato and watercress. Serve at once, straight from dish.

Cook's Notes

TIME
Preparation and cooking of this tasty dish take 20 minutes.

ECONOMY
Red or pink salmon can be used with equally good results, or canned tuna or mackerel can be used instead of the salmon. Do not use the drained oil but add 2 extra tablespoons milk to the sauce in stage 2 instead.

SERVING IDEAS
Put the salmon and macaroni layer into 4 individual flameproof dishes and serve it with a green salad.

● 490 calories per portion

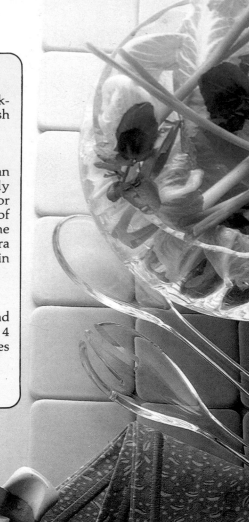

Herring salad

SERVES 4

 ½ lb salt herring fillets, drained (see Buying guide)

 2 large waxy potatoes, cooked (see Watchpoint)

1 large beet, cooked (see Buying guide)

1 large dill pickle

1 large crisp green apple

2 tablespoons mayonnaise

6 tablespoons plain yogurt or dairy sour cream

1 Cut the herring fillets, potatoes, beet and the pickle into small dice and place in a large bowl (see Preparation). Pare and core the apple and cut it into small dice. Add to the bowl (see Serving ideas).

2 Mix the mayonnaise and yogurt together until well blended and smooth. Pour over the chopped ingredients in the bowl and mix thoroughly until everything is well coated.

3 Cover the bowl with plastic wrap and refrigerate for several hours, ideally overnight, before serving.

Cook's Notes

 TIME
Preparation, including boiling the potatoes and beet, takes 1½ hours, plus chilling time.

 BUYING GUIDE
Any salt herring is suitable for this salad. Pickled rollmops in jars, or herrings canned in wine are available from delicatessens and good supermarkets.

Buy a ready-cooked beet from the supermarket, to cut down on preparation time.

! WATCHPOINT
Do not overcook the potatoes — they should be firm.

PREPARATION
Make sure the ingredients are cut into small dice for this salad — the flavors will mingle more easily.

SERVING IDEAS
You can serve as a main course, with a green salad and French bread.

Salt herring fillets have a strong, distinctive flavor, and you may prefer not to mix them into the salad. Combine the other diced ingredients as in stages 1 and 2, then roll the drained fillets up tightly and arrange around the dish, as in the picture.

● 365 calories per portion

Creamy pasta with tuna

SERVES 4

¾ lb pasta shapes (see Buying guide)
salt

6 tablespoons butter or margarine
1 small onion, chopped
1 clove garlic, crushed (optional)
2 tablespoons all-purpose flour
1¼ cups chicken broth
⅔ cups dairy sour cream (see
   Variations)
freshly ground black pepper
2 cups (about ¼ lb) button
   mushrooms, quartered
1 can (about 14 oz) tomatoes,
   drained and roughly chopped (see
   Economy)
1 cup grated Cheddar cheese
1 can (about 7 oz) tuna, drained and
   flaked

SAVORY BUTTER
6 tablespoons butter
2 tablespoons grated Parmesan
   cheese
2 tablespoons finely chopped
   parsley

1 Preheat the oven to 375°. Set a large saucepan of salted water over high heat to boil.
2 Make the savory butter: Cream the butter with the Parmesan cheese and parsley. Put the savory butter inside a piece of folded waxed paper and shape into a cylinder. Pat the ends to flatten and neaten and twist the ends of the waxed paper. Chill in the refrigerator while you prepare the pasta.
3 Add the pasta to the pan of boiling water and cook for 10-12 minutes, or according to package directions, until tender yet firm to the bite. Drain well.
4 While the pasta is cooking, melt 4 tablespoons of the butter in a saucepan, add the onion and garlic, if using, and cook over gentle heat until soft but not colored. Sprinkle in the flour and stir over low heat for 2 minutes until straw-colored. Remove from the heat and gradually stir in the chicken broth.
5 Return the pan to the heat and simmer, stirring, until thick and smooth. Reduce the heat and stir in the dairy sour cream. Remove from heat and season to taste with salt and pepper. Cover and set aside.
6 Melt the remaining butter in a small saucepan, add the mushrooms and cook for 2-3 minutes.
7 Add the tomatoes to the sauce with the mushrooms and grated cheese. Stir in the cooked pasta. Put the tuna fish in the base of a large ovenproof dish. Spoon the pasta over the tuna.
8 Cut the chilled savory butter into 8 slices and arrange them over the top of the pasta. Cook in the oven for about 15-20 minutes until the dish is piping hot.

Cook's Notes

TIME
Preparation about 45 minutes, cooking in the oven 15-20 minutes.

VARIATIONS
If sour cream is not available you can use ⅔ cup natural yogurt instead, or light cream with 1 teaspoon lemon juice added.

FREEZING
The dish can be made up to the end of stage 7 and frozen for 1 month without the savory butter. To serve: Defrost at room temperature, add the savory butter and cover with foil. Reheat in the oven preheated to 400° for 20 minutes, remove the foil and continue cooking for a further 20 minutes or until heated through.

BUYING GUIDE
Choose pasta shapes such as shells that will hold the sauce readily. Pasta rings would not be suitable for this dish.

ECONOMY
Reserve the juice from the tomatoes for use in another dish, such as a beef casserole.

● 925 calories per portion

Crab-stuffed tomatoes

SERVES 4
8 large tomatoes
about ¾ lb canned or frozen
   crabmeat (see Buying guide)
grated rind of 2 lemons
¼ cup lemon juice
2 tablespoons thick mayonnaise
4 tablespoons cottage cheese, sieved
1 bunch of watercress, chopped with
   stems removed
salt and freshly ground black pepper
few drops of hot-pepper sauce

1 Slice off the top of each tomato and set aside. Using a grapefruit knife or teaspoon, gently scoop out the flesh and seeds, taking care not to pierce the tomato shells (see Economy). Turn them upside down on paper towels and leave them to drain while you prepare the crab filling.

2 In a bowl, mix together the crabmeat, lemon rind and juice, mayonnaise and sieved cottage cheese (see Cook's tip). Lightly stir in the watercress and season to taste with salt, pepper and the pepper-sauce. Cover the bowl and chill the mixture in the refrigerator for 1-2 hours.

3 Spoon the crab mixture into the tomato shells, filling them as full as possible without letting the mixture run down the sides of the tomatoes. Carefully replace the tomato tops on the crab stuffing and serve the tomatoes at once.

Cook's Notes

 TIME
Preparation takes 30 minutes. Allow 1-2 hours for chilling the stuffing.

 SERVING IDEAS
These stuffed tomatoes are very versatile: They make an unusual appetizer for a dinner party, or may be served as a main meal with a mixed salad and French bread. For a tasty supper dish, serve the tomatoes on circles of fried or toasted bread, garnished with watercress.

 BUYING GUIDE
Canned and frozen crabmeat is sold in varying weights according to individual brands. Exact weight of crabmeat is not critical for this recipe as the size of the tomatoes will vary as well.

 ECONOMY
Discard the seeds and use the scooped-out tomato flesh for sandwiches.

 COOK'S TIP
If you find the flavor of crab rather strong, use less crabmeat and add more cottage cheese when you are mixing the filling.

 **VARIATION**
Tomatoes may be stuffed with all sorts of mixtures. Substitute drained, mashed tuna fish for the crabmeat in this recipe. Or try mixing equal quantities of cream cheese with sieved cottage cheese and adding some chopped shrimp or chopped walnuts. You can also try lime juice instead of lemon juice.

● 140 calories per portion

Roes on toast

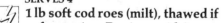

SERVES 4

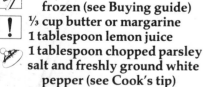

1 lb soft cod roes (milt), thawed if
   frozen (see Buying guide)
⅓ cup butter or margarine
1 tablespoon lemon juice
1 tablespoon chopped parsley
salt and freshly ground white
   pepper (see Cook's tip)
4 large slices bread, crusts removed

TO GARNISH
lemon slices, halved
parsley sprigs

1 Drain the cod roes on paper
towels.
2 Melt the butter in a skillet, add the
roes and cook fairly briskly for 3-4
minutes, turning the roes several
times to brown. !
3 Add the lemon juice and parsley
and season with salt and pepper.
4 While the roes are cooking toast
the bread, cut and arrange the slices
on a warmed serving dish. Spoon
a portion of roes with the buttery
juices onto each slice of toast (see
Serving ideas).
5 Garnish the top of each serving
with lemon slices and parsley sprigs.
Serve at once.

Cook's Notes

TIME
This dish takes only 10
minutes to prepare.

COOK'S TIP
Use white pepper in
pale-colored dishes:
Black pepper spoils the color of
the finished dish.

WATCHPOINT
Soft roes break up easily
and need careful cook-
ing in a non-stick pan.

SERVING IDEAS
Broiled rolled slices of
bacon may be served
with the roes.

BUYING GUIDE
You can buy canned fish
roes which are already
cooked: Simply turn them very
briefly in some melted butter or
margarine with the lemon juice
added.

● 285 calories per portion

Oriental seafood salad

SERVES 6
½ lb beansprouts
4 scallions, chopped
1 celery stalk, finely sliced
1 red pepper, seeded and cut into
    ¼-inch strips (optional)
¼ lb shelled shrimp, thawed if
    frozen (see Economy)
1 can (about 6 oz) crab meat, drained
    and flaked
6 Chinese cabbage leaves or lettuce
scallion tassels, to garnish

DRESSING
⅔ cup plain yogurt
6 tablespoons thick mayonnaise
finely grated rind of 1 lemon
1 tablespoon lemon juice
1 teaspoon ground ginger
a little salt and freshly ground
    black pepper

Cook's Notes

TIME
Preparation takes only 15 minutes plus 15-30 minutes chilling time.

SERVING IDEAS
Serve as an appetizer to a Chinese-style meal—it makes 6 servings. Follow salad with a main course of stir-fried vegetables with beef or pork strips and a bowl of rice. Shred some of the leftover Chinese cabbage and add to the vegetables.

Alternatively, serve this refreshing salad with fried shrimp crackers available from many large supermarkets.

ECONOMY
Omit the shrimp and use 1 can (about 7 oz) drained whole kernel corn instead. Or you can substitute 1 can (about 7 oz) tuna, drained and flaked, for the canned crab meat.

● 250 calories per portion

1 Combine the beansprouts, scallions and celery in a bowl with the red pepper, if using.
2 Make the dressing: Put the yogurt in a bowl with the mayonnaise, lemon rind and juice and ginger. Mix together and season with salt and pepper to taste.
3 Add the dressing to the bean-

sprouts mixture and toss to coat well, then fold the shrimp and crabmeat into the salad. Cover with plastic wrap and refrigerate the salad for about 15-30 minutes.
4 Arrange the Chinese cabbage on a serving plate and spoon the salad on top. Garnish with scallion tassels and serve at once.

Mussel omelettes

MAKES 4

2 jars (about 5 oz each) mussels in their own juice, drained, with juice reserved (see Variations)
½ cup butter
1 onion, finely chopped
2 celery stalks, finely chopped
4 tablespoons all-purpose flour
3 tablespoons dry or medium white wine
8 eggs
salt and freshly ground black pepper
2-3 tablespoons heavy cream
1 tablespoon finely chopped fresh parsley

1 Melt half of the butter in a saucepan. Add the onion and celery and cook very gently, stirring with a wooden spoon, for about 10 minutes until soft.
2 Sprinkle in the flour and stir for 1-2 minutes. Gradually stir in ⅓ cup reserved mussel juice and the wine and simmer, stirring, until thick and smooth, then stir in the mussels and enough cream to make a thick sauce (see Cook's tip). Season to taste with salt and pepper, being cautious with the salt, and stir in the chopped parsley. Leave the sauce on very low heat, stirring occasionally, while you make the omelets.
3 Lightly beat 2 eggs and season sparingly with salt and pepper. Melt 1 tablespoon butter in a skillet. When it sizzles, pour in the eggs, and cook for 2-3 minutes, drawing the edges towards the center with a fork as they cook. The omelet is ready when the center is still slightly runny.
4 Spoon one-quarter of the mussel sauce onto one-half of the omelet in the pan and fold the omelet over. Carefully slide it out onto a warmed individual serving plate and serve at once. Make the other 3 omelets in the same way serving each as soon as it is made.

Cook's Notes

 TIME
These omelets take only 30 minutes to prepare and cook.

 COOK'S TIP
The mussel mixture is very thick. Add the cream gradually until you have the sauce consistency to suit your taste.

 VARIATIONS
Use ½ lb shelled frozen mussels, thawed, and substitute milk for the mussel juice. Mussels or clams in brine can be used. They should be drained and milk used in place of the brine to prevent the sauce from becoming salty.

● 453 calories per portion

Devilled prawns and eggs

SERVES 4

⅓ lb frozen shrimp
4 eggs
1 can (about 14 oz) tomatoes
1 tablespoon tomato paste
2 tablespoons light brown sugar
2 tablespoons wine vinegar
1 tablespoon Worcestershire sauce
salt and freshly ground black pepper

1 Put the tomatoes in a saucepan with half the juice from the can, the tomato paste, sugar, vinegar, and Worcestershire sauce. Reserve the remaining tomato juice for future use in a casserole.

2 Bring to a boil, stirring well to break up the tomatoes.

3 Reduce the heat a little and simmer, uncovered, for 10 minutes.

4 Meanwhile, cook the eggs in gently simmering water for 7-8 minutes until hard-boiled.

5 Stir the shrimp into the tomato sauce and cook for a further 5 minutes. Season to taste with salt and pepper.

6 Peel and halve the eggs and place in a warmed serving dish. Spoon the tomato and shrimp mixture over them. Serve at once.

Cook's Notes

 TIME
20 minutes to prepare and cook.

 COOK'S TIPS
Adjust the consistency of the sauce before adding the shrimp. If it is too thick, add some of the reserved juice from the tomatoes. If it is too runny, boil it rapidly for about 5 minutes to evaporate some of the liquid.

Always use wine vinegar for a delicate flavor. Distilled vinegar is much too harsh in flavor for most dishes.

 SERVING IDEAS
For an appetizer, serve in individual dishes, without the rice accompaniment. For a main meal, surround with boiled rice.

 VARIATION
Use canned crab meat in place of shrimp.

● 175 calories per portion

Crab and cheese florentines

SERVES 4

1 can (about 6 oz) crab meat, drained and flaked, or the same weight of frozen crab meat, thawed
3 tablespoons vegetable oil
1 tablespoon white wine vinegar
juice of 1 lemon
salt and freshly ground black pepper
¼ lb raw spinach, trimmed, shredded
⅔ cup plain yogurt
finely grated rind of ½ lemon
1 tablespoon chopped chives
½ lb cottage cheese

TO GARNISH (OPTIONAL)
cayenne pepper
radish waterlilies (see Preparation)

1 Put the oil, vinegar and half the lemon juice into a large bowl and season well with salt and pepper. Beat together with a fork, then add the spinach and toss it with 2 forks until thoroughly coated. Use it to line 4 individual dishes.
2 Put the yogurt, lemon rind and the chives into a bowl with the remaining lemon juice and salt and pepper to taste. Mix thoroughly.
3 In a separate bowl, fork together the cottage cheese and crab meat. Fold in the yogurt and spoon onto the spinach.
4 Sprinkle with cayenne pepper, if liked, then garnish with radish waterlilies. Serve at once.

Cook's Notes

 TIME
Preparation time is about 25 minutes, but remember to allow time for radishes to soak if using them.

 VARIATIONS
Use shrimp or other shellfish in place of the crab. For a milder garnish, use paprika, not cayenne.

? DID YOU KNOW
Spinach is a rich source of iron and vitamins and is even more nutritious when eaten raw as suggested here.

 PREPARATION
To make radish water-lilies:

1 *Slice off the stalk and root ends, then with the stalk end downwards, cut 5 shallow petal shapes, cutting almost to the base.*

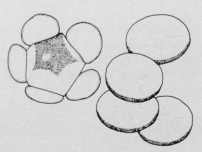

2 *Place in ice-cold water for at least 30 minutes for the petals to open. Then arrange the radish on a circle of very thin radish slices.*

● 225 calories per portion

Slimmers' crab dip with crudités

SERVES 4
1 can (about 6 oz) crab meat
⅔ cup plain yogurt
1 tablespoon chopped chives
salt
few drops of hot-pepper sauce

CRUDITES
1 red pepper
1 cucumber
3 celery stalks
2 carrots
1½ cups button mushrooms

1 Drain the crab meat and flake it into a bowl. Beat in the yogurt and chives and season to taste with salt and pepper sauce. Chill the dip while preparing the vegetables.
2 Seed the pepper and cut into strips about 2-inches long and ½-inch thick.

3 Pare the cucumber and cut into sticks the same size as the pepper. Cut the celery and carrots into the same size sticks. Halve the button mushrooms lengthwise.

4 Beat the dip again and spoon into a serving bowl. Put the bowl on a large platter and surround with the prepared vegetables. Serve at once (see Cook's tip and Serving ideas).

Cook's Notes

 TIME
Preparation takes about 15 minutes, including the chilling time.

 COOK'S TIP
The dip will separate if it is left to stand — if this happens, beat it vigorously until evenly blended again. If a smoother dip is preferred, work the dip in an electric blender before serving.

 VARIATION
Canned tuna fish or pink salmon can be used instead of the crab but they are more fattening. A 6 oz can crab meat, drained, is 145 calories; the same weight of tuna in brine, drained, is 185 calories; tuna in oil, drained, 370 calories; and pink salmon 270 calories.

 SERVING IDEAS
For an attractive display, spoon the dip into a crab shell and arrange the crudités in separate bowls.
Use savory crackers and chips instead of the vegetables, but remember that the calorie count will be higher.

● 85 calories per portion

CHEESE AND EGG DISHES

Fruit and cheese kabobs

SERVES 4

⅓ cup cream cheese
3 tablespoons seedless raisins, chopped
2 tablespoons walnuts or unsalted peanuts, finely chopped
2 oz Danish blue cheese
2 oz smoked cheese
2 oz sharp Cheddar cheese in 1 piece
1 large red apple
juice of 1 lemon
1 can (about 11 oz) mandarin orange segments, well drained, or 2 fresh mandarin oranges, peeled and divided into segments
1 can (about 8 oz) pineapple chunks, well drained
1 cup black or green grapes, washed and dried
6 lettuce leaves, shredded, to serve

1 Put the cream cheese into a bowl with the raisins and mix well. Roll into 8 small even-sized balls.

2 Spread the chopped nuts out on a flat plate and roll the balls in them. Transfer to a plate and refrigerate while you prepare the other ingredients.

3 Cut the Danish blue cheese into 8 even-sized cubes. Repeat with both the smoked cheese and the sharp Cheddar cheese.

4 Quarter and core the apple, but do not pare it. Cut in even-sized slices and immediately squeeze the lemon juice over them to prevent discoloration.

5 On 8 individual skewers, spear 1 cream cheese ball and 1 cube each of Danish blue, smoked and Cheddar cheeses, interspersed with apple slices, mandarin orange segments, pineapple chunks and grapes. Serve 2 skewers per person on a bed of shredded lettuce.

Cook's Notes

TIME
Total preparation time is about 20 minutes.

SERVING IDEAS
These kabobs make an interesting and refreshing snack or an unusual, fresh-tasting dinner party appetizer. Slices of whole wheat bread and butter go well with them, or they can be served inside whole wheat pita bread.

● 355 calories per kabob

VARIATIONS
You can vary the ingredients according to the cheese, nuts and fruit you prefer and have available; you can also add salad ingredients such as red or green pepper, chunks of cucumber, radishes or tiny tomatoes.

ECONOMY
If you have any fruit left over, tip it into a bowl and add a can of guavas for a quick fruit salad.

Cottage cheese crepes

MAKES 12
⅔ cup cottage cheese
4 tablespoons all-purpose flour
½ teaspoon salt
2 tablespoons butter, melted
3 eggs, separated
vegetable oil, for greasing

1 Preheat the oven to 225°.
2 Sift the flour and salt into a bowl, then add the cottage cheese, butter and egg yolks and mix well.
3 In a clean, dry bowl, beat the egg whites until they form soft peaks. With a metal spoon, fold 3 tablespoons of the egg whites into the cottage cheese mixture and then carefully fold in the remainder. 〔!〕
4 Heat a little oil in a heavy-based skillet. Drop about 6 table-spoons of the mixture into the pan, spacing them well apart, and cook over moderate heat for 2-3 minutes on each side until they are golden brown.
5 Remove the crepes with a spatula and keep hot in the oven while cooking the second batch. Serve at once (see Serving ideas).

Cook's Notes

TIME
The crêpes take less than 1 hour to make.

! WATCHPOINT
The air trapped in the beaten egg whites makes the mixture light, so fold them into the cottage cheese mixture very gently to avoid losing the air and making the crêpes heavy.

SERVING IDEAS
Spread the crêpes with smoked cod's roe pâté (taramosalata), available in tubs from specialty stores and deli-catessens, or with cream cheese mixed to a spread with tomato paste, chopped chives and salt and pepper to taste.

●65 calories per crêpe

Cottage cheese and ham cocottes

SERVES 4

1 cup cottage cheese
1 tablespoon vegetable oil
    1 small onion, finely chopped
2 cups chopped mushrooms
2 eggs, lightly beaten
⅓ cup diced ham
pinch of freshly ground nutmeg
salt and freshly ground black pepper
2 tablespoons butter, melted
parsley sprigs, to garnish

1 Preheat the oven to 400°.
2 Heat the oil in a small saucepan, add the onion and cook gently until it is soft.
3 Add the mushrooms and cook for 1-2 minutes only, stirring constantly. Remove the saucepan from the heat and cool.
4 Sieve the cottage cheese into a bowl and beat in the beaten eggs, a little at a time.
5 Add the diced ham to the cheese mixture with the onion and mushrooms. Add the nutmeg, then season to taste with salt and pepper.
6 Brush 4 ramekins or cocottes with the melted butter and divide the mixture between them.
7 Place on a cookie sheet and bake for about 20-25 minutes or until well risen, and brown and bubbly on top. Serve immediately, garnished with sprigs of parsley.

Cook's Notes

TIME
Preparation 10 minutes, baking 25 minutes.

VARIATION
Replace the ham with ⅔ cup shelled shrimp and the mushrooms with a small amount of canned or frozen whole kernel corn.

● 210 calories per portion

Crunchy Camembert

SERVES 4
4 Camembert triangle portions
2 tablespoons all-purpose flour
salt and freshly ground black pepper
1 large egg
3-4 tablespoons fresh white bread crumbs
¼ cup, blanched almonds, finely chopped

FRUITY SALAD
2 oranges
1 grapefruit
2 teaspoons superfine sugar
4 tomatoes, each cut into 6 wedges
1 tablespoon olive oil
1 teaspoon chopped fresh parsley
vegetable oil, for deep frying

1 Chill the cheese portions in the freezer or freezing compartment of the refrigerator for 30 minutes
2 Put the flour in a large plastic bag; season with salt and pepper.
3 Lightly beat the egg in a shallow dish. Mix together the bread crumbs and almonds and spread out on a flat plate.
4 Add the cheeses to the flour and shake until well coated. Dip them into the egg and then into the bread crumbs. Coat the portions in the egg and bread crumbs again until evenly coated. Put on a plate and refrigerate for 30 minutes.
5 Meanwhile, make the salad: Divide the fruit into segments making sure that all white pith and any pips are removed then put the segments into a bowl and mix together with the sugar. Add the tomato wedges and mix well.
6 Drain off any liquid then divide the salad mixture between 4 serving plates. Spoon over the olive oil and sprinkle with parsley.
7 Pour enough oil into a deep-fat fryer to cover the cheeses. Heat to 350°, or until a stale bread cube browns in 60 seconds.
8 Using a slotted spoon, lower the cheeses into the hot oil and deep-fry for 30-60 seconds until the coating begins to turn golden. Drain on paper towels and serve at once, with the salad (see Cook's tips).

Parsley cheese bites

SERVES 4
⅓ cup cream cheese
1 cup grated Cheddar cheese
½ cup Danish Blue cheese, at room
   temperature
freshly ground black pepper
4–5 tablespoons finely chopped
   fresh parsley
2–3 tablespoons all-purpose flour

1 Work the cheeses together with a fork to form a smooth paste. Add pepper to taste.
2 Put the chopped parsley and flour on separate flat plates. Dip your hands in the flour, shaking off any excess, then shape the cheese mixture into 20 small balls, reflouring your hands as necessary. Roll each ball in chopped parsley.
3 Transfer to a serving plate and refrigerate for 30 minutes before serving. Serve chilled.

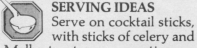

Cook's Notes

TIME
Total preparation time is only 10-15 minutes but allow a further 30 minutes for chilling.

VARIATIONS
Any mixture of cheese can be used and it is fun to experiment with different flavors, but the base must always be made from full-fat soft cheese to make the bites cling together. Try soft cheese flavored with chives and instead of Cheddar, use a grated hard cheese. A Roquefort or Italian Dolcelatte or Gorgonzola can be used in place of Danish Blue.

SERVING IDEAS
Serve on cocktail sticks, with sticks of celery and Melba toast as an appetizer or snack or add them to a cheeseboard to end a meal.

● 250 calories per ball

Dutch fondue

SERVES 4

½ lb flat mushrooms with their
  stalks, finely chopped
2½ cups chicken broth
4 tablespoons cornstarch
⅔ cup milk
½ lb Gouda cheese, finely grated
  (see Variations)
1 tablespoon finely chopped fresh
  parsley
1 teaspoon Worcestershire sauce
salt and freshly ground black pepper
mushroom slices, to garnish

TO SERVE

1 small loaf French bread, cut into
  1-inch cubes
1 lb pork sausages, fried and thickly
  sliced

1 Put the chopped mushrooms in a
saucepan with the broth and bring
to a boil. Lower the heat, cover

and simmer gently for 10 minutes.
2 In a small bowl, blend the
cornstarch to a smooth paste with a
little of the milk. Stir into the
mushroom broth, then add the
remaining milk. Bring to a boil,
lower the heat and simmer for 2
minutes, stirring all the time.
3 Turn the heat under the pan to the
lowest setting. Add the grated
cheese to the pan, 2 tablespoons at
a time, stirring well until all the

cheese has melted. Do not allow the
mixture to simmer. ⚠
4 Remove the pan from the heat
and stir in the fresh parsley and
Worcestershire sauce, with salt and
pepper to taste. Pour the fondue
into a warmed serving bowl, ⚠ or
4 individual bowls, garnish with
mushroom slices and serve at once.
Hand the bread cubes and sliced
fried sausages separately. Provide
forks for dipping.

Cook's Notes

TIME
Preparation and cook-
ing take 40 minutes.

VARIATIONS
Add ½ cup finely grated
sharp Cheddar cheese
with the Gouda, and stir 1
tablespoon dry sherry into the
fondue just before serving.

Lightly steamed broccoli
spears or cauliflower flowerets
may be used for dipping.

! WATCHPOINTS
It is vital not to allow the
mixture to simmer (no
sign of a bubble should appear
on the surface) or the fondue
will become stringy and separate and will not look as nice.

Make sure that the serving
bowl or bowls are well heated,
or the fondue will cool and
thicken around the edges.

● 665 calories per portion

Tomato, cheese and basil flan

SERVES 6-8

6 oz pie crust mix. Make up according to package directions.
4 large tomatoes (about ½ lb), sliced
1¼ cups milk
3 large eggs
1½ teaspoons dried basil (see Did you know)
¾ cup grated sharp Cheddar cheese
salt
freshly ground black pepper
a few tomato slices, to garnish (optional)

1 Preheat the oven to 375°.

2 Roll out the pastry on a floured surface and then use to line an 8-inch plain flan ring set out on a cookie sheet.

3 Arrange the tomato slices overlapping in the flan case. In a bowl, beat together the milk, eggs, basil, ½ cup of the cheese and salt and pepper to taste.

4 Pour the mixture into the flan case and sprinkle over the remaining cheese. Bake in the oven for 40-45 minutes until the filling is set and golden brown on top.

5 Allow the flan to cool for 5 minutes, then carefully remove the flan ring. Transfer the flan to a serving dish, then arrange the remaining tomato slices as a garnish, if preferred.

Cook's Notes

TIME
Preparation takes about 20 minutes, baking 40-45 minutes.

DID YOU KNOW
The flavor of sweet basil perfectly complements tomato, and this is a classic combination in many dishes, particularly those of Italian origin.

Fresh herbs are always preferable in cooking, but fresh basil is not readily available, though it can sometimes be found in specialist garden shops during the summer months.

Remember, if you want to grow basil, that it is an annual and so you will need to buy a new plant each year. It likes a sunny, sheltered spot.

There are two main kinds, with which you can experiment. Sweet basil has largish, shiny dark green leaves and white flowers. Bush basil has many small pale green leaves and tiny white flowers. Bush and sweet basil have an equally good flavor.

The strong, aromatic flavor of basil is delicious in egg, mushroom and pasta dishes, as well as with tomatoes.

SERVING IDEAS
The flan is equally good served warm or cold. It serves 6-8 as an appetizer for either a lunch or supper party. Try accompanying it with a spicy tomato relish. This tasty flan also makes perfect picnic food.

● 385 calories per portion

Stilton quiche

SERVES 5-6

6 oz pie crust mix. Make up according to package directions.
1 cup Stilton cheese, grated
⅔ cup milk
⅔ cup heavy cream
3 large eggs
2 tablespoons chopped parsley
¼ cup Stilton cheese, crumbled, to garnish (optional)

1 Preheat the oven to 400°.
2 Roll out the pastry on a floured surface and use to line an 8-inch flan ring placed on a cookie sheet. Refrigerate for 30 minutes.
3 Put the 1 cup grated Stilton, the milk, cream, eggs and parsley in a bowl and beat together, using a fork, until well blended. Pour the mixture into the prepared flan ring and bake in the oven for 40-45 minutes, until the filling has set.
4 Carefully remove the flan ring and transfer the quiche to a serving dish. Serve hot or cold, garnished with crumbled cheese if liked.

Eggs Florentine

SERVES 4

 1 lb fresh spinach
4 large eggs, hard-boiled and sliced
salt
3 tablespoons butter or margarine
1 small onion, grated
3 tablespoons all-purpose flour
1¼ cups milk
⅔ cup grated Colby cheese
½ teaspoon Dijon-style mustard
freshly ground black pepper
½ cup grated sharp Cheddar cheese
(see Buying guide)

1 Wash the spinach in several changes of water to remove all the grit. Remove the stalks and mid-ribs and discard. Put the spinach in a large saucepan with just the water that adheres to the leaves after washing. Sprinkle with salt.

2 Cook the spinach over moderate heat for about 15 minutes, stirring occasionally with a wooden spoon. Turn the cooked spinach into a colander and drain thoroughly, pressing with a large spoon or a saucer to extract as much moisture as possible. Keep hot.

3 Meanwhile melt the butter in a pan, add the onion and cook gently for about 5 minutes until soft and lightly colored. Sprinkle in the flour and stir over low heat for 1-2 minutes. Remove from the heat and gradually stir in the milk. Return to the heat and simmer, stirring, until thick and smooth. Mix in Colby cheese and the mustard, season to taste with salt and pepper and remove from the heat.

4 Preheat the broiler to high.

5 Divide the spinach between 4 individual gratin dishes. Arrange a row of egg slices on top of the spinach. Pour sauce over, covering the surface as much as possible. Sprinkle the sharp Cheddar cheese

on top of the rows of egg slices.

6 Place under the broiler for about 5 minutes or until the cheese has melted. Serve hot. (See Serving ideas.)

Egg and spinach nests

SERVES 4

½ lb spinach, stalks and large
   midribs removed, shredded
2 tablespoons butter or margarine
salt and freshly ground black pepper
4 eggs
4 tablespoons heavy cream
cayenne, to garnish
butter for greasing

1 Preheat the oven to 375°. Grease
4 individual ovenproof dishes or
ramekins.
2 Melt the butter in a saucepan, add
the spinach and cook gently for 8
minutes, or until soft. Season to
taste with salt and pepper.
3 Divide the spinach between the
prepared dishes. Break 1 egg into
each dish on top of the cooked
spinach mixture.
4 Place the dishes on a cookie sheet
and bake in oven for 10 minutes,
until the egg whites begin to set.
Remove from the oven and spoon 1
tablespoon cream over each egg.
Return to the oven and cook for a
further 5 minutes. Sprinkle a little
cayenne over each egg and serve at
once (see Serving ideas).

Cook's Notes

 TIME
Preparation 20 minutes,
cooking 15 minutes.

SERVING IDEAS
Ideal as a first course for
a dinner party or serve
with whole wheat toast for a
light lunch or supper.

 DID YOU KNOW
In France the nests are
served in cocotte dishes
— small dishes with a handle.
Cocotte dishes hold one egg.

 VARIATIONS
Place 4 tablespoons
chopped cooked mush-
rooms or asparagus in the dish
in place of the spinach.

● 195 calories per portion

Chinese egg rolls

SERVES 4

- ⅓ lb cooked chicken cut into 1-inch strips (about 1½ cups)
- ½ teaspoon cornstarch
- 3-4 tablespoons vegetable oil
- 2 tablespoons soy sauce
- 1 teaspoon sherry
- 3 celery stalks, sliced
- 8-10 scallions, sliced
- 1 cup beansprouts, well drained if canned
- 6 eggs, beaten
- 1 tablespoon water
- salt
- freshly ground black pepper

1 Put the chicken on a plate and sprinkle with the cornstarch.

2 Pour 2 tablespoons of the oil into a heavy skillet or wok. Stir in the soy sauce and sherry and heat over high heat until very hot.

3 Add the celery and scallions and toss for 2 minutes, either by lifting and shaking the pan, or using a large flat spoon.

4 Add the chicken to the pan with the beansprouts. Toss over high heat for about 1 minute, then transfer to a plate and keep warm.

5 Put the eggs and water into a bowl with salt and pepper to taste and beat until thoroughly mixed.

6 Clean the skillet with several sheets of paper towel. Add 1 tablespoon vegetable oil and heat over moderate heat. Pour in a quarter of the egg mixture, tilting the pan so that it spreads over the surface to make a thin crêpe, cook until egg sets.

7 Keep warm. Slide crêpe out onto a piece of waxed paper and place a quarter of the chicken and beansprout mixture in the middle of the crêpe. Fold in the sides and then roll up into a parcel (see Preparation).

8 Repeat with the remaining egg and chicken mixture to make 3 more egg rolls, adding more oil to the pan if necessary. Serve at once.

Cook's Notes

TIME
This nutritious appetizer takes less than 20 minutes to prepare and cook.

ECONOMY
Instead of sherry, use a little more soy sauce. Any kind of left-over cooked meat can be cut into strips and used in this recipe.

 WATCHPOINT
Do not cook the beansprouts for too long or they will go limp and lose their vitamin C content.

PREPARATION
To make the egg roll parcels:

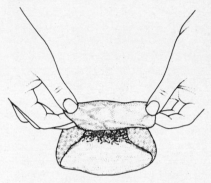

● 295 calories per roll

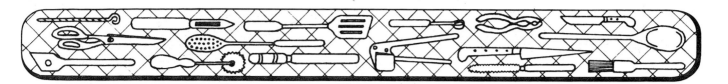

Small corn quiches

MAKES 12

 1 can (about 11 oz) whole kernel
corn, drained
 6 oz pie crust mix. Make up
according to package directions.
¼ lb bacon slices cut into ½-inch
strips
1 egg
⅓ cup light cream
salt and freshly ground black pepper
1 tablespoon fresh or dried parsley

1 Preheat the oven to 375°.
2 Roll out the pastry on a lightly
floured surface to a circle ¼ inch
thick. Cut into rounds with a 3-inch
cutter. Roll out the trimmings to
make 12 rounds altogether. Press
the rounds lightly into a muffin tin,
then refrigerate while making the
filling.

3 Put the bacon into a non-stick
skillet (see Cook's tip) and cook over
moderate heat for 3-5 minutes.
Drain on paper towels.
4 Mix the bacon with the drained
corn kernels and spoon into the
prepared pastry cases.

5 Beat the egg with the cream.
Season with salt and pepper to taste,
then stir in the parsley. Spoon
carefully over the corn mixture. ⚠
6 Bake in the oven for 20-25
minutes until the pastry is golden
and the filling firm.

Cook's Notes

TIME
The quiches take 20
minutes to prepare and
about 25 minutes to cook.

COOK'S TIP
If you do not have a
non-stick pan, heat ½
teaspoon vegetable oil in a pan
and cook the bacon.

WATCHPOINT
Make sure that the
mixture does not spill
over the edge of the pastry or
the quiches will stick.

SERVING IDEAS
Serve as a snack, or as
part of a buffet. Or
double the quantities and serve
with a salad as a main meal.

FREEZING
Cool quickly, open
freeze until solid, then
pack into a rigid container.
To serve: Thaw at room
temperature for 6 hours, then
refresh in a 375° oven for 10
minutes.

● 85 calories per quiche

Egg mousse

SERVES 4

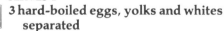

3 hard-boiled eggs, yolks and whites separated
4 teaspoons unflavored gelatin
⅔ cup chicken broth
1¼ cups thick mayonnaise, preferably homemade
1-2 teaspoons curry paste (see Did you know)
few drops of Worcestershire sauce
salt and freshly ground black pepper
1 egg white
parsley sprigs, to garnish

1 Sprinkle the gelatin over the broth in a small pan and leave for 1-2 minutes to soften and become spongy. Set the pan over very gentle heat without allowing it to boil, until the gelatin is completely dissolved ⚠ (the liquid should be absolutely clear).
2 Leave the gelatin to cool, then beat it slowly into the mayonnaise in a bowl until smooth.

3 Sieve the egg yolks and stir into the mayonnaise mixture with the curry paste and Worcestershire sauce. Chop the egg whites and fold two-thirds of them into the mixture. Season carefully with salt and pepper.
4 Beat the egg white stiffly and fold it into the mixture with a large metal spoon until evenly incorporated. Pour into an 2-pint soufflé dish (see Serving ideas).
5 Refrigerate for about 3 hours or until set. Just before serving, garnish with the remaining chopped egg white and the parsley sprigs.

Cook's Notes

 TIME
Preparation takes about 30 minutes including hard-boiling the eggs; allow 3 hours for the mousse to set.

 DID YOU KNOW
Curry paste is a blend of curry powder, oil and vinegar. It is very handy for adding to sauces and liquid mixtures, as it dissolves more readily than curry powder.

⚠ **WATCHPOINT**
If soaked gelatin is allowed to boil, it will lose its setting power. As an extra precaution, you can dis-solve gelatin in a bowl set over a pan of simmering water, but this is not absolutely necessary.

 SERVING IDEAS
An attractive way to serve this mousse, and one that is ideal for a dinner party appetizer, is to set the mixture in 4 custard cups and accompany with toast.
To serve the mousse turned out, rinse inside of dish with cold water before putting in mixture: When set, run knife around edge before unmolding onto inverted plate.

● 555 calories per portion

Cauliflower and salami soufflés

SERVES 4

1 small cauliflower, broken into very small flowerets
⅓ cup skinned and chopped salami (about 2 oz)
3 tablespoons butter or margarine
salt
3 tablespoons all-purpose flour
1¼ cups milk
pinch of freshly ground nutmeg
freshly ground white pepper
2 large eggs, separated

1 Preheat the oven to 400°. Use 1 tablespoon of the butter to grease four custard cups or ovenproof dishes.
2 Bring a pan of salted water to a boil and add the cauliflower. Simmer for 4-5 minutes, or until the cauliflower is just cooked.
3 Meanwhile, melt the remaining butter in a small saucepan, sprinkle in the flour and stir over low heat for

1-2 minutes until straw-colored. Remove from the heat and gradually stir in the milk. Return to the heat and simmer, stirring, until thick and smooth. Add the nutmeg and salt and pepper to taste, remove from the heat and leave to cool for a few minutes, then stir in the egg yolks.
4 Drain cauliflower and set aside.

5 In a clean, dry bowl, beat the egg whites until standing in stiff peaks. Using a metal spoon, fold into the sauce with the salami.
6 Arrange the cauliflower in the prepared dishes and spoon the soufflé mixture on top. Bake in the oven for 30 minutes until well risen and golden. Remove from the oven and serve at once. !

Cook's Notes

⏰ **TIME**
20 minutes to prepare plus 30 minutes cooking time in all.

❗ **WATCHPOINT**
Serve the soufflés immediately as they come from the oven as they tend to sink after a few minutes.

 VARIATIONS
Diced potatoes or parsnips can replace the cauliflower.
Use cooked bacon or left-over cooked meat like chicken instead of the salami.

🛍 **BUYING GUIDE**
There is a huge range of salami available from supermarkets and delicatessens. Both with and without garlic and including different spices, they come from many countries including Italy, Poland, Hungary and France. Any type of salami is suitable for this tasty recipe.

● 260 calories per portion

Cheese and chive soufflé

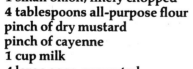

SERVES 4

1 cup finely grated Cheddar cheese
4 tablespoons butter or margarine
1 small onion, finely chopped
4 tablespoons all-purpose flour
pinch of dry mustard
pinch of cayenne
1 cup milk
4 large eggs, separated
1 tablespoon chopped chives
salt and freshly ground black pepper
melted butter, for greasing

1 Brush the inside of a 2-pint soufflé dish with melted butter. Preheat the oven to 350°.
2 Melt the butter in a saucepan, add the onion and cook gently for about 5 minutes until soft and lightly colored but not browned.
3 Sprinkle the flour, mustard and cayenne into the pan and stir over low heat for 2 minutes.
4 Remove from the heat and gradually stir in the milk. Return to the heat and simmer, stirring, until thick and smooth.
5 Remove the pan from heat, stir in the cheese, then leave the sauce to cool slightly. Beat the egg yolks, then stir them into the cheese sauce with the chives. Season well with pepper, and salt if necessary.
6 Beat the egg whites until stiff but not dry. Fold them into the cheese mixture with a large metal spoon, in a figure-of-eight motion, using the edges of the spoon to cut through the mixture.
7 Pour the mixture into the prepared soufflé dish. Run a round-bladed knife through the mixture, to make an attractive "crown" effect (see Preparation).
8 Bake in the oven for 50 minutes or until the soufflé is well-risen and golden. When lightly shaken, it should only wobble slightly. Serve at once straight from the dish.

Eggs in potato nests

SERVES 4

4 large eggs
1½ lb potatoes
1 tablespoon vegetable oil
1 large egg yolk
2 tablespoons butter or
  margarine
about ⅓ cup half and half
¼ lb mushrooms, finely chopped
  (about 1½ cups)
1 small onion, finely chopped
½ cup cooked ham, diced
1 teaspoon tomato paste
salt and freshly ground black pepper
1 small egg, beaten, to glaze
1 tablespoon chopped parsley
butter, for greasing

1 Cook the potatoes in boiling salted water until tender. Drain well and press them through a strainer. Beat in the egg yolk, half the butter and just enough of the half and half to make a firm mixture.

2 Put the creamed potato into a pastry bag fitted with a large star nozzle and pipe 4 "nests" onto a greased cookie sheet. To form the nests: Using a spiral motion, make a flat round of potato about 5 inches in diameter, then pipe a wall about 2 inches high round the outer edge. Or shape the mixture with a teaspoon.

3 Preheat the oven to 350°. Heat the oil in a skillet. Add the mushrooms and onion and cook gently until soft. Stir in the ham and the tomato paste with salt and pepper to taste, then mix well. Remove from the heat.

4 Brush the potato nests with beaten egg to glaze and spoon in the mushroom and ham mixture, dividing it equally between the nests.

5 Break 1 egg at a time into a cup and slide the eggs into the potato nests.

6 Spoon a little half and half on top of each egg to cover the yolk and dot with the remaining butter to protect the yolk during cooking.

7 Bake nests in the oven for 10-15 minutes until the whites of the eggs have just set and the yolks are still soft. With a metal spatula, carefully remove the nests from the baking sheet without breaking the egg yolks, then place them on warmed serving plates or individual dishes. Sprinkle with chopped parsley and serve at once.

Cook's Notes

TIME
Total preparation and cooking time, including boiling the potatoes, is about 1 hour.

SERVING IDEAS
Broiled tomatoes and/or chopped spinach could be served as accompaniments.

● 390 calories per portion

Cheese-stuffed zucchini

SERVES 4

4 large zucchini
salt
1 tablespoon vegetable oil
1 onion, chopped
1 cup cottage cheese, sieved
¼ cup grated Parmesan cheese
1 egg, beaten
1 tablespoon finely chopped
   parsley
freshly ground black pepper
4 tablespoons day-old soft white
   bread crumbs
½ cup grated Cheddar cheese
2 tablespoons butter or margarine
   melted
butter, for greasing

1 Preheat the oven to 400°.
2 Bring a large saucepan of salted water to a boil, add the zucchini, bring back to a boil, reduce the heat and simmer for about 10 minutes until barely tender. ! Drain and refresh under cold running water for 1 minute. Drain again.

3 Cut the zucchini into half lengthwise and with a teaspoon or grapefruit knife carefully scrape out the core and seeds from the center, leaving a good shell. Reserve the scooped-out flesh and seeds (see Cook's tip). Sprinkle the inside of the zucchini with salt, place upside down on paper towels and leave to drain for 5-10 minutes.
4 Meanwhile, chop the reserved zucchini flesh. Heat the oil in a skillet add the onion and zucchini flesh and cook over moderate heat for about 10 minutes until the onion is just beginning to brown. Transfer to a bowl and leave to cool.
5 Mix the cottage cheese with the onion and zucchini mixture. Stir in the Parmesan cheese, egg and parsley and season to taste with salt and pepper. The mixture should hold its shape: If it is too soft, add a few of the bread crumbs.
6 Grease a large shallow ovenproof dish and stand the zucchini halves in it in a single layer, skin side down. Using a teaspoon, fill the zucchini with the stuffing, heaping it in a mound on each half.
7 Mix together the bread crumbs and grated Cheddar cheese and

sprinkle evenly over the zucchini. Drizzle the melted butter over the top and bake in the oven for 25-30 minutes until golden and bubbling. Serve hot.

Egg and avocado bake

SERVES 6

6 eggs, separated
1 large avocado
6 tablespoons browned bread
 crumbs (see Preparation)
3 tablespoons vegetable oil
1 onion, finely chopped
1 clove garlic, crushed (optional)
4 tablespoons finely chopped fresh
 parsley
salt and freshly ground black pepper
¾ cup grated Cheddar cheese
melted butter or margarine for
 greasing

1 Preheat the oven to 400°. Brush 6 individual ovenproof dishes with melted butter, then coat them evenly with 4 tablespoons of the bread crumbs. Set aside.

2 Heat the oil in a skillet, add the onion and garlic, if using, and cook gently for 3-4 minutes until the onion is soft but not colored. Set aside to cool for about 5 minutes.

3 Cut the avocado in half. Remove the seed, scoop out the flesh into a bowl, then mash with a fork to a purée. Beat in the egg yolks and parsley, then the cooled onion and salt and pepper to taste.

4 Beat the egg whites until standing in stiff peaks, then fold them into the avocado mixture. Pile into the dishes, scatter remaining crumbs on top and bake in the oven for 20 minutes.

5 Sprinkle the top of the rising mixture with the cheese, then return dishes to the oven for a further 15 minutes until they are well risen and golden. Serve at once.

Salad kabobs

SERVES 4

½ small cauliflower, divided into flowerets (see Watchpoint)

1 can (about 12 oz) luncheon meat, cut into 1-inch cubes (see Cook's tips)

⅓ lb Edam cheese, rind removed and cut into ¾-inch cubes (about 1½ cups)

1 tablespoon olive oil

1 teaspoon wine vinegar

1 teaspoon chopped fresh parsley

1 red apple

2 teaspoons lemon juice

½ teaspoon superfine sugar

SAUCE

4 tablespoons thick mayonnaise, preferably homemade

2 tablespoons dairy sour cream

1 teaspoon tomato paste

½ teaspoon Dijon-style mustard

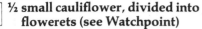

Cook's Notes

TIME
Preparation takes about 30 minutes.

WATCHPOINT
Make sure the cauliflower flowerets are large enough to thread easily onto the skewers without breaking.

SERVING IDEAS
These kabobs are also ideal for a picnic: Wrap them on skewers in plastic wrap or foil or pack in a rigid container. Put the sauce in a container with a tight lid.

COOK'S TIPS
If you chill the can of luncheon meat for 30 minutes before dicing, it makes it easier to cut.
The prepared kabobs can be covered and stored in the refrigerator for up to 1 hour.

● 560 calories per portion

---

1 Beat the olive oil, vinegar and parsley together in a bowl. Add the cauliflower, mix well and leave to stand for 5-10 minutes.

2 Meanwhile, leaving the skin on, cut the apple into 8 wedges and remove the core. Mix the lemon juice and sugar together and toss the apple in this mixture.

3 Thread the cauliflower, apple, luncheon meat and cheese alternately onto 4 long kabob skewers. Transfer to a serving plate and, if liked, use remaining pieces of apple or cauliflower to garnish.

4 Make the sauce: Beat the sauce ingredients together, then transfer to a small bowl. Serve the kabobs (see Cook's tips) with the sauce handed separately.

Spinach and Brie puffs

SERVES 4

½ lb frozen spinach, thawed and well drained (see Cook's tip)
2 oz Brie, thinly sliced (see Buying guide)
1 egg, beaten
¼ teaspoon freshly ground nutmeg
salt and freshly ground black pepper
1 sheet (½ of 17 oz package) frozen puff pastry, thawed
1 tablespoon grated Parmesan cheese

1 Preheat the oven to 425°.
2 Put the spinach in a bowl, stir in half the beaten egg and the nutmeg. Season to taste with salt and pepper.
3 Roll out the pastry on a lightly floured surface. Trim it to a 12-inch square, then cut into four 6-inch squares.
4 Divide the spinach equally between the squares, spreading it diagonally over one-half of each and leaving a ½-inch border. Top the squares with Brie slices, dividing them equally between the 4 squares.
5 Brush the edges of the pastry with beaten egg, then fold the pastry over to form a triangle and enclose the filling. Press the edges firmly together to seal them, then knock up with a knife and flute. Brush the tops with beaten egg, then use a sharp knife to make 2 small slits to allow the steam to escape. Sprinkle over the Parmesan cheese.
6 Dampen a cookie sheet and carefully transfer the triangles to it.
7 Bake in the oven for about 10 minutes, until the pastry is golden. Serve the puffs hot or cold.

Gingered eggplant dip

SERVES 4

2 lb firm eggplant, stems removed
¾ cup plain yogurt
1 clove garlic, crushed (optional)
1 tablespoon light brown sugar
1 teaspoon grated fresh ginger
½ teaspoon cumin powder
a little salt and freshly ground black pepper
fresh coriander or parsley sprigs, to garnish (optional)

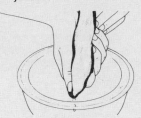
1 Preheat the oven to 400°. Prick the eggplant all over with a fork, then put them into a roasting pan and bake in the oven for 45-60 minutes, until they feel really soft when they are pressed with the back of a spoon.

2 Remove the eggplant from the oven and leave until cool enough to handle. Cut them in half lengthwise, and squeeze gently in your hand to drain off the bitter juices (see Preparation). Scoop out flesh and leave until cold.

3 Put eggplant flesh in a blender with the yogurt, the garlic, if using, sugar, ginger, cumin and salt and pepper to taste. Blend until smooth. Transfer to 1 large or 4 small serving dishes. Refrigerate for 2-3 hours to allow dip to firm up.

4 Just before serving, garnish with coriander or parsley sprigs, if liked.

Avocado and apple grill

SERVES 4

2 ripe avocados
4 crisp green apples
2 tablespoons butter
2 tablespoons all-purpose flour
1 cup milk
¾ cup grated Cheddar cheese
2 teaspoons Dijon-style mustard
salt and freshly ground black pepper
juice of ½ lemon
4 tablespoons fresh whole wheat
  bread crumbs

1 Preheat the broiler to high.
2 Make the sauce: Melt the butter in a small saucepan, sprinkle in the flour and stir over a low heat for 1-2 minutes until it is straw-colored. Remove from the heat and gradually stir in the milk. Return to the heat and simmer, stirring, until thick and smooth. Stir in ½ cup of the cheese and the mustard and season to taste with salt and pepper. Stir until the cheese has melted, then remove the pan from the heat.
3 Peel the avocados, cut in half and remove the seeds. [!] Cut lengthwise into thin slices. Pare, quarter and core the apples. Cut into thin slices. Arrange the slices of avocado and apple in layers in 1 large or 4 individual shallow gratin dishes (see Serving ideas). Squeeze the lemon juice over them immediately to prevent discoloration.
4 Pour the sauce over the avocado and apple. Mix together the remaining cheese and the bread crumbs and sprinkle evenly over the top.
5 Place under the broiler for about 5 minutes until golden brown and bubbling. Serve at once.

Cook's Notes

TIME
Preparation and cooking take about 20 minutes.

WATCHPOINT
Prepare the avocados just before they are needed as their flesh quickly turns black if exposed to the air when left to stand.

SERVING IDEAS
Serve in individual gratin dishes, this makes a most delicious first course for a dinner party. The number of servings can be easily adjusted up or down by allowing ½ an avocado and 1 apple per person — the quantity of cheese sauce remains the same for up to 8 servings.
  Swiss or Emmenthal cheese and a combination of half milk and half dry white wine would make a richer sauce for special occasions.

● 455 calories per portion

Stuffed cucumber salad

SERVES 4

1 large cucumber, cut into 24 even slices (see Buying guide)
1 head Boston lettuce, leaves separated (see Buying guide)
¾ lb carrots, finely grated
3 tablespoons golden raisins
small parsley sprigs and a few chopped walnuts, to garnish

FILLING

½ lb cream cheese
⅔ cup shelled chopped walnuts
2 teaspoons finely chopped fresh parsley
2 teaspoons chopped fresh chives or finely chopped scallion
½ teaspoon paprika
salt and freshly ground black pepper

DRESSING

5 tablespoons vegetable oil
2 tablespoons white wine or cider vinegar
large pinch of dry mustard
pinch of sugar

1 Make the filling: Put all the filling ingredients in a bowl, season with salt and pepper and mix well with a fork.
2 Remove the seeds from each slice of cucumber with an apple corer or a small sharp knife. Season on both sides with salt and pepper and set out on a flat plate.
3 Divide the filling between the cucumber slices, pressing it into the central hole and piling it up on top.
4 Make the dressing: Put all the dressing ingredients in a small screw-top jar, season with salt and pepper then shake the jar well to mix together.
5 Arrange the lettuce leaves on 4 individual plates and drizzle a teaspoonful of the dressing over each serving. Carefully transfer 6 cucumber slices to each plate, arranging them in a ring.
6 Mix the grated carrots with the golden raisins in a bowl. Add the remaining dressing. Toss to coat thoroughly, then pile into the center of the rings of stuffed cucumber slices. Garnish 3 cucumber slices on each plate with a parsley sprig and 3 slices with a few chopped walnuts. Serve at once.

Cook's Notes

 TIME
Preparation time is about 45 minutes.

 BUYING GUIDE
Choose a straight cucumber so that it will be easy to slice evenly.
A curly, soft-leaved lettuce is best for this recipe because it gives an added attraction, but any soft-leaved lettuce will do.

 SERVING IDEAS
Serve the stuffed cucumber slices, with the lettuce as a garnish, as a tasty starter or with drinks. As an alternative suggestion, the salad could be accompanied by cold, sliced meat to make a much more filling supper or lunch.

 VARIATION
Use chopped muscatel raisins instead of golden raisins.

● 410 calories per portion

Eggplants on waffles

SERVES 4

2 large eggplant, cut into cubes
salt
2 tablespoons vegetable oil
1¼ cups beef broth
4 teaspoons tomato paste
2 cloves garlic, crushed (optional)
½ teaspoon dark brown sugar
freshly ground black pepper
4 waffles
¾ cup grated Cheddar cheese
coriander sprigs or parsley, to
    garnish

1 Layer the eggplant cubes in a colander, sprinkling each layer with salt. Put a plate on top and weight down. Leave to drain for about 30 minutes to remove the bitter juices. Rinse under cold running water, pat dry with paper towels or a clean dish cloth and set aside.

2 Heat the oil in a large skillet, add the eggplant, broth, tomato paste, garlic, if using, and sugar. Season with salt and pepper.

3 Bring to a boil, then lower the heat, cover the pan and simmer for 8-10 minutes, stirring frequently, until the liquid is absorbed and the eggplant cubes are tender.

4 Meanwhile, preheat the broiler to high and toast the waffles for 4 minutes on each side or cook as directed on the package.

5 Place the waffles in a flameproof dish, pile the eggplant mixture on top and sprinkle over the grated cheese. Broil for 1-2 minutes (see Cook's tip).

6 Garnish waffles with coriander sprigs or parsley and serve at once.

MEAT DISHES

Bacon and onion crispies

SERVES 4

- 4 slices lean bacon, chopped or diced
- 1 small onion, chopped
- 3 tablespoons butter or margarine
- 3 tablespoons all-purpose flour
- ⅔ cup milk
- 1 teaspoon dried mixed herbs
- 1 egg, lightly beaten
- 1 cup fresh white bread crumbs
- vegetable oil, for deep-frying

1 Melt the butter in a small saucepan, add the bacon and onion and cook them over moderate heat for 3-4 minutes.
2 Sprinkle in the flour and stir over low heat for 1-2 minutes until straw-colored. Remove from the heat and gradually stir in the milk.
3 Return the pan to the heat and cook for 2-3 minutes, stirring all the time until very thick and creamy. Remove from the heat and leave to cool.
4 Stir the herbs into the mixture, divide into 8 equal portions, then form each portion into a ball (see Preparation). Put the egg and bread crumbs in separate shallow dishes.
5 Roll each ball in the egg, then coat with the bread crumbs.
6 Heat enough oil to cover the balls in a deep-fat fryer to 350° or until a stale bread cube browns in 60 seconds. Add the balls to the oil a few at a time and deep-fry for 2-3 minutes until golden brown on all sides.
7 Drain the crispies on paper towels and serve at once.

Cook's Notes

 TIME
Preparation takes about 20 minutes, cooking 5 minutes.

 PREPARATION
The mixture will be very soft: Use your finger-tips to form it into ball shapes.

 COOK'S TIP
The crispies should have a delicious crisp coating and a soft center.

 SERVING IDEAS
Make double the quantity and serve as an appetizer snack with drinks.

● 465 calories per portion

76

Saucy ham and shrimp rolls

SERVES 4

8 slices cooked ham (½ lb)
¼ lb package parsley and thyme
   stuffing mix
½ cup shelled, chopped shrimp,
   thawed if frozen
parsley sprigs, to garnish

CHEESE SAUCE
¾ cup grated Cheddar cheese
2 tablespoons butter or margarine
2 tablespoons all-purpose flour
1 cup milk
pinch of freshly ground nutmeg
½ teaspoon prepared English
   mustard
salt and freshly ground black pepper

1 Preheat the oven to 400°.
2 Make the stuffing according to package directions. Allow to cool slightly and mix in the shrimp.

3 Divide the stuffing between the ham slices, spooning it in a strip about 1½ inches from each edge. Starting at the edge nearest the stuffing, carefully roll up each slice of ham. Place the shrimp-filled ham rolls, with the join side down, in a shallow ovenproof dish, large enough to hold them in one layer.
4 Make the sauce: Melt the butter in a saucepan, sprinkle in the flour and stir over low heat for 1-2 minutes until straw-colored. Remove from heat and gradually stir in the milk. Add the nutmeg and mustard and season to taste with salt and pepper. Return to the heat and simmer, stirring, until thick and smooth. Remove the pan from the heat and stir in half the grated Cheddar cheese.
5 Pour the sauce over the ham rolls and sprinkle with the remaining cheese. Bake in the oven for 20 minutes until the sauce is golden and bubbling. Garnish with parsley and serve at once straight from the dish (see Serving ideas).

Bacon kabobs with peanut dip

SERVES 4

¾ lb bacon in one piece, trimmed and then cut into ¾-1 inch cubes
3 tablespoons crunchy peanut butter
⅓ cup shredded coconut
⅔ cup water
salt and freshly ground black pepper
coriander leaves, to garnish

MARINADE
2 tablespoons vegetable oil
2 teaspoons curry paste
2 teaspoons lemon juice
½ teaspoon ground coriander
¼ teaspoon ground turmeric

1 Make the marinade: Blend the marinade ingredients in a bowl.
2 Add the meat cubes and coat thoroughly in the marinade. Cover and leave to stand for 30 minutes.
3 Preheat the broiler to moderate.

4 Remove the meat cubes from the marinade with a slotted spoon. Reserve marinade. Thread the bacon pieces onto each of 12 wooden toothpicks (see Cook's tip).
5 Broil the kabobs for 10 minutes, turning occasionally, until cooked.
6 Meanwhile, pour the reserved marinade into a saucepan and add

peanut butter, coconut and water. Season to taste with salt and pepper and heat through gently, stirring constantly until well mixed.
7 Arrange the bacon kabobs on a warmed serving plate and garnish with coriander. Serve at once with the dip handed separately in a warmed bowl (see Serving ideas).

Cook's Notes

 TIME
Preparation and cooking take 25 minutes plus 30 minutes marinating.

 COOK'S TIP
Soak the toothpicks in cold water for 30 minutes to prevent them from becoming too brown when broiling the meat. Or, if wished, small metal skewers may be used instead.

 VARIATIONS
Use either pork steaks or picnic ham in place of

the bacon.
   To make a tomato dip for the bacon, heat the marinade with 1 can (about 10 oz) condensed tomato soup with ¼ cup water added to it.

SERVING IDEAS
For an unusual party platter, arrange the bacon kabobs on a serving plate in alternating rows with peeled cucumber strips. Garnish with coriander, put dip in a coconut shell and place on the plate.

● 280 calories per portion

78

Chicken fritters

SERVES 4

1 cup boneless cooked, skinned and finely chopped chicken
2 tablespoons butter
3 tablespoons all-purpose flour
⅔ cup milk
1 egg yolk
⅓ cup cooked, finely chopped ham
4 button mushrooms, finely chopped
½ teaspoon dried oregano
salt
freshly ground black pepper
¼ lb package batter mix
6 slices of bacon
vegetable oil, for deep frying

1 Make the sauce: Melt the butter in a saucepan, sprinkle in 2 tablespoons flour and stir over heat for 1-2 minutes until straw-colored. Remove from heat and gradually stir in the milk and the egg yolk. Return to heat and simmer, stirring, until thick and smooth.

2 Stir in the chicken, ham, mushrooms and oregano and season to taste with salt and pepper. Pour the mixture onto a large plate, spread it out with a knife and leave until completely cool, about 15-20 minutes.

3 Make up the batter according to the package directions. ⚠

4 Stretch each of the bacon slices with the back of a knife and then cut them in half.

5 Divide the chicken mixture into 12, then roll each piece into a ball, and shape it into a roll. Wrap each roll with bacon.

6 Spread out the remaining tablespoon flour on a flat plate and season with salt and pepper. Dip each roll in the flour until evenly coated.

7 Heat the oil in a deep-fat fryer to 375° or until a day-old bread cube browns in 50 seconds.

8 Dip the rolls one at a time into the batter, then drop into the hot oil and deep fry 6 at a time for about 6 minutes until golden and crispy.

9 Drain on paper towels and keep warm while cooking the second batch. Serve at once.

Cook's Notes

 TIME
Preparation, including cooling, takes about 40-45 minutes. Cooking takes 12 minutes.

 SERVING IDEAS
Serve the fritters with a crisp green salad, or for a more substantial dish, serve with a tasty rice salad.

⚠ **WATCHPOINT**
Follow the package directions for making batter for frying as opposed to batter for pancakes. No egg is required for the batter.

● 505 calories per portion

Curried chicken salad

SERVES 4

1 lb boneless cooked chicken, skinned and cut into 4-inch strips

⅔ cup thick mayonnaise, preferably homemade

⅔ cup plain yogurt

1 teaspoon curry paste (see Cook's tip)

juice of ½-1 lemon

2 red apples

4 celery stalks, chopped

4 scallions or 1 small onion, finely chopped

¾ cup green grapes, halved and pitted

½ cup shelled, coarsely chopped walnuts

salt and freshly ground black pepper

1 small lettuce, shredded

Cook's Notes

TIME
Preparing the salad takes about 20-25 minutes.

COOK'S TIP
This quantity of curry paste will give a mild-flavored dressing for this salad. Increase the quantity a little at a time, tasting as you add the curry paste, if you prefer a hotter flavor.

SPECIAL OCCASION
Decorate the salad with a little whipped cream and top with a few walnut halves. Alternatively, garnish with watercress.

VARIATION
Use a can (about 8 oz) of pineapple pieces, drained, instead of grapes.

● 590 calories per portion

1 In a bowl, mix together the mayonnaise and yogurt. Mix the curry paste with the juice of half a lemon and fold into the mayonnaise mixture.

2 Core and slice but do not pare the apples and mix them into the mayonnaise mixture with the celery, onions, grapes and walnuts.

3 Add the chicken strips to the mixture turning them to coat evenly with the mayonnaise. Taste and season with salt and pepper if necessary, and add more lemon juice if liked.

4 Arrange the lettuce in individual dishes. Pile the salad on top and serve at once.

Peanut drumsticks

SERVES 4

8 chicken drumsticks, skinned (see Preparation)
⅓ cup smooth peanut butter
1 egg, beaten
⅓ cup milk
salt and freshly ground black pepper
about ½ lb plain potato chips
½ cup all-purpose flour
vegetable oil, for greasing

1 Preheat the oven to 375°. Brush a cookie sheet with oil.
2 Put the peanut butter into a bowl and beat in the egg with a wooden spoon. Gradually beat in the milk, then season to taste with salt and pepper. Pour the mixture into a shallow bowl.

3 Put the potato chips into a plastic bag and crush with a rolling pin. Spread out on a flat plate.
4 Spread the flour out on a separate plate.
5 Coat each chicken drumstick in flour, then in the peanut mixture

followed by the crushed chips. Make sure that each layer is evenly covered.
6 Place the coated drumsticks on the prepared cookie sheet and bake in the oven for 45-50 minutes, or until crisp and lightly browned. Serve hot or cold.

Cook's Notes

 TIME
Total preparation and cooking time is about 1 hour.

 VARIATIONS
Crunchy peanut butter can be used instead of smooth. Dried bread crumbs or crushed cornflakes can replace the crushed potato chips.

● 590 calories per portion

 PREPARATION
To skin the drumsticks, cut through the skin lengthwise with a sharp knife or scissors, then pull the skin away with a sharp tug.

 SERVING IDEAS
Serve hot with buttered noodles or baked potatoes, or cold with an endive and cress salad or as part of a finger buffet with a relish.

Savory bacon fritters

SERVES 4

about ½ lb lean bacon slices, (see Buying guide)
1 cup all-purpose flour
2 teaspoons dry mustard
large pinch of celery salt
large pinch of paprika
freshly ground black pepper
2 eggs, separated
½-⅔ cup beer
1 tablespoon vegetable oil
1 onion, finely chopped
½ green pepper, seeded and chopped
vegetable oil, for deep-frying
tomato wedges, to serve

1 Sift the flour into a bowl with the dry mustard, celery salt, paprika and pepper to taste. Make a well in the center, add the egg yolks and beat to mix thoroughly, gradually working the dry ingredients into the center. Beat in enough beer to make a batter with a thick coating consistency.

2 Cover the bowl with plastic wrap, then set aside in a cool place for 2 hours (see Time).

3 Broil the bacon until cooked but not crisp. Drain on paper towels, then cut into 1-inch lengths.

4 Heat a little oil in a skillet. Add the onion and pepper and cook gently for 5 minutes until the onion is soft and lightly colored. Remove with a slotted spoon and add to the bacon.

5 Pour enough oil into a deep-fat fryer to come halfway up the sides. Heat the oil gently to 375°, or until a stale bread cube turns golden in 50 seconds.

6 Meanwhile, in a clean dry bowl, beat the egg whites until they are standing in stiff peaks. Using a large metal spoon, carefully fold the egg whites into the batter with the bacon, onion and green pepper.

7 Drop a few tablespoonfuls of batter into the hot oil and deep-fry for 3-4 minutes, until puffed and golden brown. Drain well on paper towels and keep hot while frying the remainder, but remember to reheat the oil between each batch.

8 Serve with tomato wedges.

Cook's Notes

TIME
Preparation, 20 minutes, cooking 15 minutes, and 2 hours for batter to rest. To save time, use milk instead of beer and rest it 30 minutes.

BUYING GUIDE
Collar slices are lean and less expensive than back bacon; they are ideal for this recipe.

SERVING IDEAS
Serve with a selection of relishes, and with a colorful white and red cabbage coleslaw.

●595 calories per portion

INDEX